Shalom My Love

The story of a true love
that bridges heaven and earth

Sunny Ariel

SAPPHIRE
HOUSE

Cover Graphics and Book Design by
Aryeh Swisa and Janet Morrell
Back Cover Photograph by Debra Montgomery

Cover art portrays a universal symbol of the
dawning of peace, love and prosperity for planet
earth as created by Rainbow Crossing, Inc.
Posters can be purchased by calling 1-800-521-0737

First edition 1998
Copyright ©1998, Sapphire House
P.O. Box 609, Lafayette, CO 80026-0609

ISBN # 0-932-48290-2

1. Ariel, Sunny.   2. Creative non-fiction.   3. Spirituality
4. Relationships.   5. Death and dying.   6. Title

Printed in the United States of America by
Gilliland Printing, Inc., 1-800-332-8200

Our deepest fear is not that we are inadequate.

Our deepest fear is that we are Powerful beyond measure.

It is our light, not our darkness, that frightens us.

*We ask ourselves, Who am I to be brilliant, gorgeous,
talented and fabulous?*

Actually, who are you Not to be?

You are a child of God.

*There's nothing enlightened about shrinking so that
People won't feel insecure around you.*

*We were born to make manifest the Glory of God
that is within us.*

*It's not just in some of us; it's in everyone.
And as we let our light shine, we unconsciously give
other people permission to do the same.*

*As we are liberated from our own fear, our presence
Automatically liberates others.*

— Nelson Mandela
1994 Inaugural Speech

In Gratitude

"When the student is ready, the teacher will appear"...

I am deeply indebted to the teachers who have inspired me with the desire to discover and unfold the divinity latent within me: Nava Timor, Dawne Kovan, Rand Lee, Arthur Molinary, Beth Hin, Robert Griffin, Richard Casey, Jacquie Hobbs, Marilyn Rodack — and Ammachi.

To Harlan and Peter, I had no idea how tranformational a Rocky Mountain high could be until I moved to Colorado and connected with you guys. Thank you both for your goodness and generosity of spirit. Onward and upward.

Thank you Martin, Gadi's earth brother, for helping me through my rough patches. Aryeh, your God-given gift of graphic design has made this book beautiful. Thanks, Debra, your soul shines through your camera lens. Rebekah, thank you for helping with the final stages of this book... 'she is within you...' David, your compassion and patience has helped me more than you will ever know. May the blessings you have given me return to you a thousand-fold. Thanks, Leonard, the Rabbi different in the City Different. To my German and Austrian friends, Uli, Ursula, Mike and Wulfing: thank you, you bring your compassion straight through your hearts. To Jerry who has conversations with God every day, God bless you. To Ellen in Santa Fe, Maita in Denver and Rick in Manchester, a blessing on your 'kops', mazel tov.

To Deb in Vancouver, giant kudos to you! You took my original manuscript and gave it form, structure, and magic. You are an angel! And also dear Debby of Ram Pages, I couldn't have done it without your help.

Author's Note

This is my story as it unfolded. In order to protect the privacy of most of the people involved, I've changed their names. I've also had a series of extraordinary experiences in the process of bringing this book to print, two of which I'd like to share with you.

One occurred while I was struggling for weeks to compose a foreword. Suddenly, late one night, I "heard" Gadi telling me that he wanted to write it. I also knew that he did not require me to change his name. After all, he no longer has an ego... so Gadi has contributed to the foreword of this book.

The second experience occurred while the final corrections were en route to the printer. Shortly before mailing them off I had met a young woman named Jacquie, a psychic from Manchester, England. After setting up about twenty-five psychic readings for her, I was delighted to learn that it was finally my turn.

Jacquie went into trance, then told me I had many lives in the Holy Land, that there is wisdom in the Kaballah for me, that Gadi is strongly with me, and that I need to meditate regularly and ask to be shown the light of my Jewish heritage. "There's a small book in the Bible called Habakkuk", I said. "And for years I've been drawn to the verse in which God tells Habakkuk to 'write the vision and make it plain upon stone tablets, so that those who read it may understand it clearly.' " "Yes, yes," she said, "they're all here." "You are the stone tablet. It's as if you are being written upon. You were of the same time. I know this is going to blow you away, but you were one of the original writers of the Bible! You are to be a spokesperson for them." She added that if I meditate and then read the Bible, I will be able to rewrite the spiritual words, since I came to embody the wisdom of the past.

Alas, I was not Cleopatra, or Helen of Troy, or even the Queen of Sheba, but rather some less stellar character destined to transcribe old words for new times.

I decided to give it a try. If I could find a Biblical verse for each chapter that would resonate with the energy of that particular chapter, I would change some of the existing quotes to words of ancient wisdom.

I meditated.

Then I opened the Great Book and began to read. It was all there — words long frozen in the heavens were crying to be released into the receptive warmth of an awakening planet. Another veil had parted, and I could almost hear Gadi laughing and saying: "Holy craziness! You go, girl." That I trust, is the message of this book. I hope you find it comforting, healing, and empowering.

Sunny Ariel
Lafayette, Colorado

Table of Contents

Foreword

This is quite a moment for you and for me. You are ready to bring out our story. It is important that people understand the dynamics of what has occurred. Anyone can communicate with a loved one on the other side (we call your side "the other side") so long as they are open to the different ways in which this can happen.

In your case you write down the words you "sense" that you are hearing me speak. You allow your mind to be free so that you can tune in to me. Other people have dreams, which are very real ways of communicating with our side. Sometimes there is a recognized smell, like when your daughter smelled her pop-pop's aftershave on the first anniversary of his passing.

We are all with you — if not in body, then in spirit, in heart and in consciousness. It is important to recognize that we need your open hearts to be a bridge to us so that you can cease to be afraid and come to realize that death is only a transition into another dimension and nothing to fear. You have beautifully explained this in your book.

Know that we who have passed over look to those of you reading this book with great love and appreciation. We want to be acknowledged for the light beings we are — and we are here to help the loved ones we have left behind. Please ask for our help and it will be given to you. In dreams . . . in sudden insights . . . in songs . . . in rainbows . . . in the skies . . . and in a breathtaking sunset.

Together we can co-create a situation which brings you closer to us and us closer to you. And in doing so the veil between our side and your side is lifted, along with the fear of death.

To anyone who is reading this who has a loved one on this side, please trust the power of these words: *No one you love ever dies.*

Gadi Danzig
October 1, 1998

Prologue

Then Saul said to his servants, "Seek out for me a woman who is a medium, that I may inquire of her." And his servants said to him, "Behold, there is a medium at Endor."

I Samuel 28 : 7

Samuel, the first of the prophets of later times, is a forerunner of Saul, the first of Israel's kings, and he acts as counselor and judge. Samuel, not necessarily an ecstatic visionary but rather an interpreter of the present has, by the time of the above scripture, died. King Saul is desperate: the Israelites and the Philistines are about to clash once again, and Saul fears the enemies' numbers. He inquires of the Lord, but the Lord does not answer him through the usual dreams, prophets, or Urim and T'umim, the sacred oracles. In fear and desperation, he instructs his servants to find a woman medium, and they tell him of the woman at Endor. The stories and legends of the Jewish people at the time of the First Temple took place in the great valley of the Galilee where Endor is located.

Saul, according to the story, had banished all the mediums and wizards from the land. Therefore, he disguises himself and goes to see the woman at night, accompanied by two servants. He asks her to "divine for him a spirit" and bring up whomever he names. In fear she responds: "Surely you know what Saul has done, how he has cut off the mediums and wizards from the land. Why then are you laying a snare for my life to bring about my death?" (I Samuel 28 : 9)

Saul swears that no harm will come to her, and he asks that she bring up Samuel from the dead. By this time, however, she recognizes the king, and she is even more beside herself. She does as she is commanded, and an old man wrapped in a robe begins to rise from the depths of the earth.

Samuel, not at all pleased that his time in Sheol, the land of the dead, has been disturbed, bickers with Saul and ignores the king's distress. Saul is miserable: God has left him, he says, and he asks Samuel for advice with the Philistine matter. Samuel retorts with, "Why then do you ask me, since the Lord has turned from you and become your enemy?" He goes on to seal the fate: the Philistines will defeat Israel, and Saul and his sons will die. "Tomorrow," says Samuel, "you and your sons shall be with me."

Saul falls on the ground in a fit of despair, and Samuel's spirit vanishes. The woman comforts Saul and makes haste to feed him, to give him the best of what she has: her calf and her bread, her compassion and kindness overshadowing the caustic Samuel, who seems to delight in bearing ill tidings. Saul returns to his camp in low spirits, aware that the fate of the battle and his own fate have been sealed...

My story, as true as the Bible story, begins not 3000, but eight years ago. Not Saul, the King of Israel, delivered into the hands of the Philistines, but my lover Gadi Danzig, delivered to meet his Maker in the Philippines when the helicopter from which he is filming crashes. No Witch of Ein Dor am I, although I did often console Gadi with home-baked chocolate chip cookies. Just before his trip to the Philippines, Gadi asked me to take him to meet with an Israeli psychic or medium for a reading. That session is the pivot for this story. Gadi, during the session, spoke of the source of life being the fear of death. It was only after he died that I was able to begin to come to terms with our relationship and come to understand that Gadi's death was the ultimate sacrifice of one individual who was, while he was alive, totally unaware of his soul's mission.

Living in Israel, a Levantine country and, in many respects, a man's country, was not easy for me, and yet I loved it with an inexplicable passion. My love for Gadi throughout our peripatetic relationship was, nonetheless, unconditional love.

After his death, the full extent of his duplicity became clear, and in trying to understand the reasons I had chosen this particular relationship, I embarked on a spiritual path which would take me from Israel, with its raging intifada, to the mesas of northern New Mexico, to the green grass of England, to magical Vancouver, British Columbia, and to Colorado's front range where all the dots of my life finally begin to connect. My journey has revealed to me a large body of evolving human beings who are awakening to their spirituality, and from Gadi I have come to understand that we must move in harmony if we are to heal ourselves and our planet.

Not one of us is here by accident — there are no coincidences. If you are reading this book, it is almost a certainty that you are awakening too. Perhaps you, like me, are coming to the realization that we are all spiritual beings in a physical body. If our story can help you, even in the smallest way, to understand your magnificent spiritual heritage, if our story of love and enlightenment transcending death gently helps you to remember your own starry origins and your own exalted self, then you, too, are participating in the raising of consciousness, as part of the preparation for a better world.

                    Didn't We?
This time we almost made
some sense of it, didn't we, love?
This time we almost made the pieces fit,
didn't we, love?
This time we held the answer right in our hand
- then we touched it and it had turned to sand.
This time we almost made it to the moon,
didn't we, love?
This time we almost sang our song in tune,
didn't we, love?
This time we almost made our poem rhyme,
this time we almost made the long, hard
climb...

    ...didn't we almost make it this time?
                                    — Jim Webb

1

Opening the Door

There's an old Sufi story about the lover who comes to the dwelling of the Beloved and asks to be admitted. "Who is there?" the Beloved asks, and the lover answers, "I am here." But the Beloved refuses to admit the lover, who then wanders for years in grief and longing, finally returning to the Beloved and begging to be admitted.

"Who is there?"

"You alone are there," the lover responded. And the door was opened.

I guess that I started, tentatively, to open my door—just a crack—in 1989. I'd been living in Israel since 1978, and the intifada* was beginning to polarize an already overly polarized country. Magical Saturday treats of baklava and mint tea in the bazaars of Jerusalem's Old City were no longer considered safe for non-Arabs, and I had left "Jerusalem the Golden" for Tel Aviv, "the city that never sleeps." In truth, it wasn't the intifada that got me out of Jerusalem — it was Gadi.

When we first met in the early 80's — I was producing a promotional film for a hotel and Gadi was sent to direct and shoot it — I think I understood for the first time the meaning of the phrase, "the eyes are the windows of the soul." The chemistry was definitely there, but not the timing. I was living with Manny, and Gadi was married. By 1989 we had been seeing each other for four years — Manny was no longer in my life, and Gadi had left home.

I had become friendly with a woman named Miriam, an ex-kibbutznick who worked as a psychic, or medium. Since February 7, 1989, was Gadi's 45th birthday and he was busy shooting *Green Fields*

* *Palestinian political/militant uprising movement of the 1980's*

(a feature film about the futility and pain of the intifada), he invited me to spend a couple of days with him at a kibbutz guest house near Jerusalem. Before leaving Tel Aviv for London, I asked Miriam to "channel" a birthday message for Gadi. I gave him the transcription, but he put it away and we had no discussion about it, so that, a couple of weeks later when he asked me to set up an appointment for him to meet with Miriam, I was quite taken aback. Whatever came through must have had quite an impact. Sometime in March we went to Miriam's together and had a session which lasted about two hours. Actually, it's not fair to say that *we* had a session. It was Gadi's session and, looking back, I understand that it was a "cosmic set-up" and that I was destined to be there that day.

The information that came through Miriam in trance was extraordinary: "There are many moments of soul searching and loneliness which today are quite strong, and the feeling is that you somehow have to break away from the circle you are going around in. You are quite aware — this doesn't mean that you do anything with your awareness. With you, it's a long process — the awareness, putting it all together — when those things happen you have to do something — you can't then stay in the same place. Your lack of confidence manifests itself into thinking that if you make a major change in your life and you don't succeed, you will be left without anything, and it is this fear that is stopping you from making changes . . ."

But it was Gadi himself who surprised me by suddenly saying, "Listen, I can tell you that I don't believe there is such a thing as death — the soul continues on, I believe it — I even wrote a script about it — but the fact is, we don't know much about this."

Miriam, who by this time had come out of her trance, said, "Do you know how very much proof there is? Gadi — there's so much we can talk about; we've worked on souls for years."

Gadi replied, "Well anyway, the source of life is the fear of death."

I couldn't figure out what he was saying. Did he mean that our fear of death is so powerful that it motivates our lives?

He continued: "About once a year I get into bed with the fear of death — it passes within half an hour. I assume this happens to everyone. When I get into a car or do my army reserve duty, then I'm afraid that something will happen to me — that I'll die. I ask the driver to drive slowly, carefully...when I go to the army, I'm one of the soldiers who doesn't sleep all night. I say, 'Just me the fucking terrorists will get'...but, when I go up in a helicopter, I'm reborn. I'm not afraid of anything...I ask the pilot to do the most dangerous things — I generally hang out of the chopper. Lots of people tell me how frightened they are that their plane will crash while they're airborne — I don't feel that way at all. I had an experience in the Congo three years ago in a small plane through a lightning storm — my assistant cameraman prayed to God...OK, this is it, goodbye kids — the plane flew wherever it wanted to...night...storm... lightning... we knew it was the end. I wasn't frightened even for one second. OK, I said — we'll die, so we'll die. Something that doesn't happen to me on the ground." And then Gadi suddenly added, "In any event, none of us will be able to enjoy our next incarnation because we don't have enough awareness yet."

Miriam answered, "So start being aware. Do things now. Start to investigate, to question, to read. Becoming aware doesn't just happen one-two-three."

Then Gadi said something that really made no sense at all at the time: "Sunny can continue the work."

At the very end of the taped session, Miriam said that she got a picture of an upside-down forest where there was a ball and Gadi was going around together with the ball. She told him that he thinks there is something else, but that all he needs to do is pick up the ball. She continued: "I'd like you to read the information we received regarding awareness and male/female relationships — we get it from the spirit guides — we work on the information for a few years. We get data about the Earth, the stars, general information on souls...when a person dies...information on that soul...information..." and here the fourth side of the tape ended. Soon afterward, Gadi went to the Philippines to film a documentary with an Italian production company, and was due to return in two weeks.

I had a friend visiting London for ten days, and I asked her to bring me Linda Goodman's latest book, *Star Signs*. I had a weird feeling that this book had some meaningful relevance for me. Linda Goodman is, of course, best known as an astrologer, but her *Star Signs* couldn't be further from astrology. It's all about the harmonics of the universe, how everything — words, colors, numbers — is connected. The chapters on anagrams and numerology are first-rate. I was particularly drawn to the chapter on numerology. I would learn much more about it later, but at the time I just knew that her system of numerology worked.

Naturally, the first name I "checked out" with the system was Gadi's. His name came to 12-"the Sacrifice; the Victim." What is particularly interesting about the numerological system Linda Goodman uses is the advent of compound numbers that go from 10 to 52; it is the compound number that gives us an excellent karmic description — a kind of "soul reading."

There was Gadi in Manila; the two weeks had already become six, and he seemed to have cut himself off — from me, at any rate. I consoled myself by listening to the taped session with Miriam. It was his voice, after all, and a far sight cheaper than trying to track him down on location. Anyway, I'd been sending him psychic messages to hurry home so that we could find a different spelling for his name to negate "the Sacrifice; the Victim," but I guess he hadn't tuned in.

On the tape, right after he talked about how he felt "reborn" whenever he was in a helicopter, he asked Miriam about a script he had written called *Children of Immortality* and "if the day will come when this story, which is a fantastic project, will happen — and if this happens, I have no doubt that this will be the 'headline' which comes after many years of dreams in my life." Miriam's response was especially interesting — she actually repeated the information three times.

She said: "According to what seems to be and according to the feeling, this can be a project which you can do and which will be very successful; it looks like the beginning won't be easy — but afterward, it will open up into two directions — even into a direction which you cannot imagine — it looks like a major point in your life that if you go for it, your soul is your engine and that is what makes it truly genuine. Despite the difficulty which will take place in the beginning, it looks as if you can really go for this. Go ahead with it — somehow this project has a totally different nuance to it. It looks really good. It can bring much success and will go in directions which you haven't even thought of — a real breakthrough. This project has lots and lots of strength, and you will receive help with this…it looks as if the beginning will be difficult, but afterward, there will be a huge breakthrough."

I had sat in on many of Miriam's individual sessions, often as a translator, as well as attending her workshops, and was convinced that she was channeling really "high level" stuff. Nothing astral at all. Miriam worked with about twelve different guides and, although she had never actually "seen" them, she did describe their different personae to me. The only one who seemed to know when "they" were present was Pumpkin, my cat. He would roll and purr on my rosewood dining room table whenever Miriam was over – that is, until my cousin, Pippa, came over one evening.

She never met Miriam prior to that evening; all she knew about her was that she was a medium. Suddenly, as Miriam was in trance, Pippa leaned over and whispered to me, "There's a tall, somber-looking male holding a sceptre, next to your dining room table, and a short, fat, jolly type on the table where Pumpkin is rolling around." Exactly two of the guides Miriam had described to me! We were six people that evening, and we were all in a state of shock, particularly Pippa, who had never "seen" before this, and most definitely Miriam who, after working with her guides for years, was finally able to have them authenticated by an outside observer. We asked Pippa to draw what she had seen, and Miriam started to resemble Pumpkin had he swallowed a canary as she watched Pippa drawing.

I, too, have been given a divine gift, although only recently have I truly begun to understand and appreciate it. I have been receiving "information" through automatic writing since 1977. I just need to sit down with a writing pad and pen, silence myself for a few moments and take some deep breaths, and I will start to get one word at a time, which I write down.

Back in 1977, I was part of a weekly metaphysical group that met once a week in Philadelphia. It was run by a woman named Joan who used to channel and access the Akashic records. I'd never even heard of the Akashic records. I was the youngest member of the group, and although I understood very little, I was impressed with it. One evening Joan received a message that the group needed a physics equation and that I would be able to give it to them. I laughed and said, "Impossible!" The last science course I'd studied was biology in the ninth grade. The group was not interested in my excuses and told me to take a pen and paper and go into the next room and sit quietly for five or ten minutes. I felt very foolish for a good number of minutes, and then I received something. I honestly thought that I'd "made it up," but one of the group members was a physicist and he said that I'd given them exactly what they needed. I figured that they were just humoring me, or perhaps they were all little nuts.

The following year I moved with my then six-year-old daughter to Israel, where I continued to do automatic writing, though not on a regular basis; and quite honestly, even though I am able to write for people I've never met, I never took it all that seriously.

So, on the 9th of May, 1989, when Gadi had been away for six weeks, I got the following from my automatic writing:

Know this: All that we have been telling you these years is coming to pass now. You felt a distant chord sound within you when you read Linda Goodman's book, regarding your relationship with Gadi. Know this: He will soon return, and we have done our best to bring him to the point of understanding so that he will now be able to come to you and work together with you on both the relationship and a project. We call him 'Luck',* and he will join hands with you, and together you will accomplish glorious things. Be mindful of jealous and ill-intentioned people. You must see that your relationship is needed for both of you to complete the final karmic round, for your love will generate great miracles both with each other and for the world. Soon you will know of what we speak.

* I had been given the name 'Luck' several years before I met Gadi. I actually wrote 'Luke,' but later I discovered that the Hebrew word 'Gad' means luck.

I was elated with this information. Gadi had promised me I could produce *Children of Immortality*, and I was close to producing another film that I had asked Gadi to direct. Although we were not living together, I felt certain we soon would be.

A week later, I got a phone call from my friend Robin, who said she had a terrible premonition that something awful had happened. She told me she would wait a few hours and then call her family in the States to make sure everything was OK. Soon after, I received a call from Judi, who said that she had woken up in the night in a cold sweat from a horrible nightmare. I asked her what she dreamed, and she said, "The number two." We checked in a book of dream symbols and read: "The number 2 symbolizes the end of a relationship." Since Judi was not in a relationship at the time, we were both puzzled.

That afternoon I felt awful and knew something was horribly wrong, but I had no idea what it could be. I felt as if all the energy had been zapped out of me. At 11:30 that evening, I received a call from a producer friend in London — he was one of the few people in the profession who knew about my relationship with Gadi. The helicopter which was filming *Delta Force II* had crashed near Manila. Gadi had joined the crew and gone up as cameraman at the last minute. Gadi was killed instantly; four others died after getting to the hospital. I later read in *Premiere Magazine* ("Death in the Philippines," December, 1989) that the entire production was run about as unprofessionally as anything could be run, that Chuck Norris had had a similar accident just the year before, that they had rented a helicopter (the only one they could get) which had been impounded and had not been flown for over a year, and that the pilot, who also died, was not a stunt pilot. I was in a state of shock.

Gadi, as beautiful as Jeff Bridges and Mel Gibson combined — Gadi of the wonderful body no longer had a body — Gadi, who only felt safe in helicopters and in bed with me, had "passed over." I went back to the automatic writing of the previous week and slowly began to comprehend. Miriam called me the next day and said she was feeling that Gadi wanted to come through and may she come over. What transpired that afternoon proved to me, beyond any shadow of a doubt, that there is no death...

When I was still a youth, before I went traveling, in my prayers I asked outright for Wisdom....

"Poem on Quest for Wisdom"
(found at Qumran and Masada)

Hear, my daughter, the ordinance of your father, and forsake not the law of your mother; For they shall be an ornament of grace for your head and a necklace about your neck.*

Proverbs 1: 8,9.

*All the Biblical verses are from the *Holy Bible*, ancient Eastern text, translated from the Aramaic by George M. Lamsa, (Harper, San Francisco)

11

Spirit and Family

For children in America, it is traditional to make a wish on the first star. My wish as a little girl was always the same... I wished that I would never die. I imagine that death frightened me very much when I was a child. I had lost a brother when I was two, and Michael's death was something that was never discussed at home, but I knew how he died. It was in Wallasey, England, a small coastal town across the Mersey from Liverpool, and my mother had put him in the pram with cushions behind his head. We were going to the photographer's studio to have his picture taken. He was six weeks old. As we were leaving the house the telephone rang, and my mother asked me to keep an eye on Michael, saying that she would be back soon. I remember waiting and waiting and finally I went into the house to get her and when we came out he had managed to turn around in the pram and had suffocated.

Two years later, on the date he had been born, my sister was born. My mother always believed that Michael had come back to her, and I always felt guilty that I had been responsible for the death of the only son in an Orthodox Jewish family that would eventually boast three daughters.

During my 28th year something occurred that would change my life. It was during one of those Sunday afternoon family gatherings, when everyone is lazing about after a typical American-Jewish brunch. My Uncle Morris, the brilliant American GI my Aunt Betty had married in England (and the reason that my parents and their two small daughters had immigrated to the USA), was speaking about his early childhood in Russia. His parents had been shot in front of his eyes during a pogrom. The youngest of seven brothers and sisters who all managed to come to America, my uncle was raised by them. That Sunday he said that seeing death at such a tender age had no affect on him. My kid sister, the family's self-appointed psychologist, said, "Of course it did — every event in childhood, particularly during the first five years, is crucial to the development of the person's subsequent feelings of self-worth. Children of that age can't think, they only feel."

I was reminded of the story of the little girl who comes home from pre-school with a finger painting. "What a beautiful picture and what a clever girl you are," her mother says, and hangs the picture on the wall. The next day the child is looking at it and remembering the good feelings she had when Mother made such a fuss over her and her picture. Now she will really make mummy happy. Taking her finger-paints from her cupboard she paints the biggest, most beautiful picture on her wall. So pleased is she, in fact, that she drags her mother by the hand into her room to see the masterpiece. Suddenly the child is told: "What a naughty girl you are! Look what a terrible mess you've made on the wall," and, more likely than not, she is smacked and sent to bed without supper!

When Mandy said that small children can't think, that they can only feel, I said that I had always felt guilty that I had, by leaving him unattended, caused the death of my brother Michael. "What are you talking about?" my mother asked.

"Well, you know," I said, "if I hadn't left him alone in the pram he wouldn't have died."

"What are you talking about?" my mother said again. "He wasn't in a pram, he was in the garden… as a matter of fact, you came up to the kitchen and told me that Michael was crying, but when I looked out the window he wasn't crying, and it was only a little while later that we noticed that he had stopped breathing. It was crib death."

For twenty-six years I had believed that I had been responsible for the death of my brother. I know that my parents grieved terribly and then, suddenly, the subject was closed. Why did I invent a story that was so real to me that I never felt the need to question it? It is significant that this startling revelation occurred during my 28th year, which is usually the time we experience our Saturn return.

The planet Saturn has suffered from a bad reputation, always cast as the "heavy" in the chart. Saturn is the teacher whose class is the toughest, but whose lessons are well-learned. And, although the tests of Saturn come at regular seven-year "exam periods," the "final exam" comes at around 28. Saturn is a planet which illuminates our fears, our hang-ups and our important lessons in life and is concerned with our maturity and with what we need to know in order to survive in the world. I had never questioned the pram story. It happened and that was why, I believed, my brother had died. Now I had to do some heavy-duty soul-searching to figure out why I had invented this fantasy, how it had affected twenty-six years of my life and, most importantly, how this new revelation would change my life. Years later Rand Lee, a psychic in Santa Fe, during a past-life reading said, "The role of the death child in others' lives sends out ripples to everyone it touches."

My Aunty Vera from Manchester, who recently passed over at the age of 89, told the story — again and again — of how I stayed with her when my mother went to give birth to Michael. Nobody seems sure of just how long this was, but it was a good few weeks. The story goes like this: Aunty Vera brought me home and stayed for tea and scones in the garden. When it was time for her to leave, so they tell me, I began to scream and cling to her, shouting: "Don't leave me, Aunty Vera; don't leave me with her," pointing to my mother. During all the family Passover Seders, both in England and in America, throughout years of weddings, bar mitzvoth and other family gatherings, this story has been told and retold and nobody, including me, understood the significance.

A little girl, two years old — the youngest child in a family of cousins all much older, an especially beautiful child who has been doted upon by all and sundry, whose mother actually feels a personal affront if passing strangers don't stop and tell her how gorgeous her child is — has not only been separated from her mother for several weeks, which probably seem like eternity to her, but when she returns home there is a new baby boy, upon whom everyone is doting. There is also the normal jealousy (although my mother tells me that I adored Michael and in the same sentence tells me how she would never nurse him in front of me so I wouldn't be jealous). A few short weeks later, she obviously senses something is wrong and tries to tell her mother that the baby is crying; and her mother, who is rushing to get ready to go out that evening, looks out the window and sees that the baby isn't crying at all. Suddenly there is no more baby and everything is hushed up. Is it so surprising that she blames herself and creates a story which is her only defense in dealing with her confused inner-child?

The truth is that my childhood memories don't begin for me until I am about four-and-a-half and on the ocean liner which brought us to America. I do understand today that my mother did the best she knew how to do, and even more importantly, I truly believe that we choose the childhood circumstances we most need for the growth of our soul. But often our interpretations, as vulnerable children, of our pressures, hurts and traumas, compel us to close ourselves down in order to protect our inner child. As adults this hurting inner child is still within us — blocking our potential, our power and our right to happiness and success.

This concept of the soul's choosing parents came into full focus when my own daughter, Rachel, was about fifteen. I went into her bedroom of our Tel Aviv flat to find a book (in itself a major feat, what with the uncluttered floor space measuring all of 6 square inches — even Pumkin the cat would not set his fastidious paws in her room) and saw, next to the book, her diary wide open on her desk. Afterward it hit me that her open diary had not tempted me in the least, which was amazing to me because my own mother, bless her, had real issues with trust, particularly when I was a teenager.

My mother, who was unable to talk to me then and was convinced that I was being much naughtier than I actually ever was, used to read my diary and my mail as well as listen in on my phone conversations. So, seeing and not reading Rachel's diary showed me why I had chosen my mother (with her lack of trust) so that I could remember that feeling and be presented with the key of trust in my relationship with my own daughter.

My friend Barbara and I were talking about the soul choosing the parents. She asked her five-year-old son, Alexander, if he had chosen her to be his mummy and he said, "Yes, I chose you because you are so

lovely," and Barbara and I both knew intuitively that he was remembering on a soul level. Another friend tells me that his daughter told him
right before her sixth birthday, "I looked down from heaven and saw you
and Mummy and then I came down." When I discussed this concept
with Rachel, she was about twelve. We were having a bit of a row over
something or another. She must have said something particularly nasty
because I said, "You know, they say the soul chooses the parent, so even
though you might not accept it, you chose me to be your mother." She
thought for a few seconds and then said, "Maybe so, but in a past life
you can be sure that *I* was the mother and *you* were the child."

When we can look at our childhood and genuinely understand that
everything that happened to us was a soul choice that each of us made
in order to learn the lessons we need in our lives, and when we can
assimilate this into a "gnosis" or a divine "knowing" and understand
that we cannot change anyone but ourselves, and that people we
relate to are mirrors of aspects of ourselves, and that we reincarnate
with the same people again and again in order to learn our lessons —
then we reclaim our power, release our fears and rekindle the harmony
within ourselves.

In the year of my Saturn return, slowly I began to see how I had
chosen many things in my life because I saw myself as a person who
had caused the death of her brother. Because I didn't feel especially
worthy, I chose a husband who in many ways reminded of my mother.
Once I came to understand the dynamic behind the marriage, I was
able to release it. The marriage lasted only five years and, if indeed
Rachel chose me as her mother, she also chose her father for the
lessons she needed to learn in her life. The Spiritual Laws say that we
not only choose our parents, we also choose our life's drama... that we
see the whole film before we come down. (I used to joke that when I
was shown the film I wasn't paying attention because I was busy flirt-
ing with the angel sitting next to me!)

After the divorce I decided (obviously following the script) that I
wanted to raise my child in Israel. We lived there for twelve years. I
went there as a Zionist and left there as a masochist, but already well
on the path that would change my life, as well as the lives of many others I was yet to meet.

Look down from thy holy habitation, from heaven, and bless thy people Israel and the land which thou hast given us, as thou didst swear to our fathers, a land that flows with milk and honey.

Deuteronomy 26:15

111

Land of Milk & Honey

ה "I'll tell you why I'm optimistic. Sadat arrived in Jerusalem on a Saturday night. I was very moved by Sadat. I watched history at its best, an exalted moment of history. And I cried. But I didn't only cry because of Sadat. I was moved by the way he was received by my brothers and sisters in Israel. These same Israelis who, three or four years earlier, had suffered because of Sadat, received him with open arms. There were many orphans, many widows in the crowd, women who lost their husbands, their sons, their brothers, in a war that Sadat had unleashed on the eve of Yom Kippur in '73. And yet it was enough for Sadat to come to Jerusalem on that Saturday evening–that Sabbath evening — for the people to undergo a real metamorphosis."

— Elie Wiesel

"Here's where I see the great grace of God. I think that Sadat transcended himself as did the Jewish people. I suspect that when Sadat started his journey, he wasn't at all sure he was going to go as far as he went. And I think that God lifted him up out of himself. And I think that the reception that he was given in Israel was a kind of lifting up by God. God is the ultimate peace."

— Cardinal John O'Connor

A Journey Of Faith by Elie Wiesel and Cardinal John O'Connor
Donald I. Fine, Inc., New York, 1990

Strains of *Rowan and Martin's Laugh-In* when Goldie Hawn was just starting to make an impact on the national comedy scene...Art Carney saying to Lily Tomlin, "What's a nice kid like you doing in a place like this?"...or "It's a nice place to visit, but you wouldn't want to live there"...or perhaps Judy Carne's "flying fickle finger of fate" probably all sum up my love/hate relationship with the state of Israel. During the many years I lived there, I was saying, "And now folks, it's sock-it-to-me time." And yet, until I fell in love with Gadi, I could honestly say that I had never loved any man as much as I loved that convoluted and eclectic little country. The film *Exodus* and Paul Newman certainly contributed to the fantasy — the first time I went to Israel, I was a nineteen year old ostensibly on her way to her junior year of college at the Hebrew University, but all the while secretly searching for Ari ben Canaan, aka Paul Newman.

Growing up in Philadelphia, I had the opportunity to see many Broadway shows on their trial runs before opening in New York. The musical *Milk and Honey* was one such show. It was a soppy story about a group of Hadassah ladies who go to Israel and fall in love with beautiful, big and brawny Israeli men who, of course, live on a kibbutz and wear only shorts and sandals. The title song from the show was "...this is the land where the hopes of the homeless and the dreams of the lost survive and — this lovely land is mine." I was hopelessly hooked. Growing up as the daughter of a "shochet," or ritual slaughterer, it was understood — was it ever understood — that if I ever married a non-Jew, my father would sit *shiva* for me; in other words, I would be 'dead' for him, and he would observe the traditional seven days of mourning. So Israel seemed a good compromise — practically everyone was Jewish and practically all the guys were gorgeous.

In November 1977, a travel agency in Philadelphia which was my PR client invited me on a free ten day trip to Israel. We arrived at exactly the same time that Anwar Sadat made his historic peace mission to Jerusalem. I was deeply moved by the synchronicity of Sadat and my visit and decided then and there to move to Israel with my daughter. There was a passionate and electrifying energy there which enthralled me. I felt that finally I had come home where my dark curly hair, pretty face and goddess-like body were in vogue.

In 1986, a year after Sadat's assassination, I came across an interview in *People* magazine with Jehan Sadat. She said her relationship with her husband was ongoing, that he visited her at night. Ten years later I would be saying the same thing about Gadi.

My very dear friend Mira has lived in Israel since she was twenty-one. She's one of the country's leading astrologers and a very funny lady. She grew up in Canada where, she says, all the hottest guys were Fonzie look-alikes, but she wasn't allowed to date those Italian hunks. Then, she says, she came to Israel and all the guys looked exactly like the guys she wasn't allowed to date in Canada, but now it's OK — they're Jewish. So she married a Jewish guy from Kurdistan. After a few years of marriage, she realized that although he may have looked like Robert de Niro, he acted more like Stalin.

Israel is a Levantine country and, although the strides made in science and technology are incredible and Tel Aviv rivals Los Angeles with its choice of restaurants, shopping, and nightlife, make no mistake about it: this is the Middle East. Well over half the Jewish population hail from Arab countries, and Israel has its internal prejudices and decidedly cultural differences, and ultra Orthodox and secular Jews have violent demonstrations over Sabbath driving. It is, therefore, a country of strong polarities. I met the best people in the world there — and the worst.

Israelis can be arrogant or aggressive, and they have a pressing need to be "au courant," to buy the latest thing, to be seen at the newest exhibition, to constantly judge and be certain that they know everything better than anyone else. I remember going into a children's clothing store in Jerusalem when Rachel was nine because I'd seen an adorable jumpsuit in the window. I asked the salesman to show me the size 8 and the size 10, and I saw that the size 8 would fit her perfectly. "How old is she?" the salesman asked. "Nine," I replied. "Well then, you must buy the size 10." Never mind that it was miles too big for her, he insisted that I buy her that size and was really piqued and practically refused to sell me the size 8!

And yet, there is something inexplicably addictive about Israel (like buying a tub of Ben & Jerry's Coffee Heath Bar ice cream that should last a week…and lo and behold, it's one a.m. that night — and the tub is empty!) Incidentally, Ben & Jerry opened their first ice-cream shop in Tel Aviv on Dizengoff Street in 1989 (luckily for me, it was within walking distance from my flat). I don't recall any advertising, and certainly the Vermont-based Ben & Jerry's was not known in Israel, yet after just a couple of weeks, people were lined up in the streets to buy the latest American import, "Vanilla with Gold Drops."

When I ran an advertising agency there, a timeshare company asked us to handle their newest project in Eilat. We prepared a detailed proposal including print, direct mail, and radio advertising. The client said that all our hard work had been unnecessary, that he was hoping to recapture the phenomenal success he'd had in timeshare sales in a sister project in Tiberias. With no advertising whatsoever, they had managed to sell more timeshare units in a three-month period than any other place worldwide.

"How was that possible?" I asked (after all, I was Madison Avenue-trained), to which he replied that all he had done was buy a share himself and then tell a friend. Within a few short weeks, Israelis all over the country were saying to one another, "What? You haven't bought a unit yet? I have."

Everyone in Israel has this need to jump on the bandwagon and for me, coming from America, I found it sometimes funny and often very sad. I remember once, years ago in the States, there was talk that the cost of coffee would rise by a few cents. By the next day, everyone stopped buying coffee, and by the following day the price increase was shelved. In Israel, when the price of coffee is about to be raised (or sugar, oil or whatever), Israelis rush to the supermarkets and empty the shelves of the endangered product.

So it is not surprising that every self-help course, every newest pop psychology seminar and, of course, many New Age workshops find their way to the pliant atmosphere of Israel. EST, IAM, Hari Krishna, Jews for Jesus, the Mormons, Physical Immortality — these are just some of the groups that have had wide followings. I recall hearing from the Physical Immortality people that, outside of "Lalaland" (California) their largest membership was in Israel. One reason, I think, that this happens is due largely to the fact that Israelis are totally group-oriented — their group follows them through nursery school, primary school, high school, youth groups and, most important, the army. They are, in may aspects, a nation of followers.

Some years ago, on Israeli Independence Day, I was a guest at my friend Shifra's kibbutz. A few hundred kibbutznicks were sitting in the dining room where a movie screen had been set up, and slides with the words to the old pioneer songs (e.g., "We have come to the Land to build and to be built...") flashed on the screen. The perfunctory accordion player was there, and everybody was singing the oldies-but-goodies from the Israeli hit parade, 1948–1967. They were singing from their throats, that's for sure, but I sensed a blockage around their hearts. I suddenly felt that if I had stood up and said "follow me," then all the people in that dining room would have blindly gone to wherever I might have led them. It was a sobering moment.

I, too, had been lured into the Zionistic, idealistic dream. After all, hadn't Theodor Herzl, that enigmatic Austrian Jew and the Father of Zionism, said, "If you will it, it is no dream," and hadn't that motto become the cornerstone for the founding of the modern state of Israel in 1948? Enlightened folk today know very well that what you think, you become, and in many ways Israel is a dream come true. I used to believe that the tremendous victory of the Six Day War in '67 gave an entire generation of Israelis such a sense of power and control that this attitude seeped into every crevice of the country, from politicians to my landlord; everybody is a prime minister.

Another reason that so many young and thirty-something people in Israel continue to run after the latest so-called panacea for all their spiritual lacks is the fact that most have grown up without a dream. The "Zionist dream" of their parents' generation has no relevance for them. I only need to think of Rachel's friends from her high-school years — what a creative, bright, sensitive and evolved group they were — and realize that they have recently completed three years of army service — three years, for some, of being stationed in the West Bank, having to protect themselves and the settlers there from frustrated stone-throwing young Arab boys.* When we are able to acknowledge our weaknesses, we can use them as catalysts for taking action to change and improve ourselves and those around us. This is a group of kids with the planet Pluto in Libra (1973–1982 and part of 1971) and a generation which is just beginning to assert itself.

The planet Pluto, often called "the private eye," governs with the underside of our personality, digging out our secrets to effect a total transformation, and nothing is sacred. Discovered in 1930, Pluto is the farthest planet and takes about 234 years to orbit the sun; therefore, only seven signs have felt its presence in this century. My daughter's generation was born into a time of landmark legislation on life-or-death issues such as abortion and euthanasia; the ERA, AIDS, and gay rights movements. Marriage is being redefined as an equal partnership, and parental roles are being shared. How different this is from those who were born when Pluto was in Cancer (May 28, 1914–June 16, 1939), when motherhood, security, and the breast became fetishes for this generation; it was also the time of the rise of women's rights, dictators who swayed the masses with emotional appeals, and the rise of nationalism. Rachel's grandparents' generation is deeply sentimental and places great value on emotional security and, since this generation also lived through the depression and the Second World War, financial security also is high on the list.

It can be a great help in understanding our parents, children and, of course, ourselves once we become aware of the magnificent harmonics of the Universe and how each and every one of us a special note that is integral to the harmony of the planet.

When my father died in 1993, I flew to the States to be with my mother during the traditional Shiva, or seven days of mourning. My mother was understandably in great grief. My dad had died suddenly, while working, the day before their fifty-first wedding anniversary. My father, a supervising rabbi for the Union of Orthodox Congregations, would have left my mother well provided for, I thought. Actually, it was my mother who always dealt with the family finances, dabbling with mutual funds back in the early seventies, and she was always the one in the family with a "head for money", although since her marriage she

* All of Rachel's friends served during the years of the intifada

hadn't worked outside the home. After the Shiva, I came back to England, and Rachel came with me.

I'd been back for a few weeks when I received a short note from my mother which said, "Enclosed is a list of the monies you have received from your father." There was a breakdown of everything my parents had ever given me — I mean from Rachel's tap dancing school when she was three years old to the AT&T answering machine they brought to Israel (as a birthday present, I had been told at the time).

It was true that we had been having a terribly difficult time during our last few years in Israel, and my parents had often been helpful during some very lean and hungry times, but I never imagined that my mother had kept a list — down to the exact cent — of every single time Dad had helped us. I thought that if someone offered me five thousand dollars to account for every penny I'd ever given Rachel, I'd have to forfeit the offer. I wasn't in a position during those years to give as much to my daughter as I would have liked to, but I always gave unconditionally when I was able, and good times or bad, I never kept a list.

When I told friends about the list from my mother, they were shocked and surprised and said that she had done an awful thing. Julia said that it was typical of Jewish families–why, in her family her mother could tell you who ate ten extra strands of spaghetti twenty-three years ago! But my British "soul therapist" friend Diana Cooper, author of *A Time for Transformation* (London Bridge) said, "This is her way of telling you how much they love you." That resonated with me immediately. For my mother's generation, with its emphasis on motherhood and security, this would be her way of showing me how much I was loved. I sent her a letter letting her know that I understood why she had sent me the breakdown, and for the first time since my father had died, she communicated with me in a warm and loving way.

My generation, which is also Gadi's, has its Pluto placement in Leo (June 16, 1939–August 19, 1957). Paramount to our generation is self-expression (we, after all, invented rock and roll). The transformative power of this Pluto in Leo is apparent in the rise of television and the development of the entertainment business. We were the generation that "did our own thing" and advocated freedom of sexual expression.

But I believe that my daughter's generation (with Pluto in Libra) will start to be more and more at the forefront of effective action. These are the young men and women today who truly believe that they can make a difference. They connect to the present plight of the environment, to the number of species going extinct every day, and to the growing hole in the ozone. They can and do look at the big corporations and those of us who are driving cars, and know that we owe it to the Earth to recycle more, drive less — and they really get involved. When Rachel was seventeen, she announced, one day, that the thought of how all animals suffer when they are killed made her decide to become a vegetarian — as did many of her generation.

When she was a small girl, she actually loved steaks (I can imagine her saying "ugh, how gross" were I to remind her!). Rachel had always been an aspiring and (although the opinion is her mother's) talented actress. She even worked with the world-famous violinist Itzhak Perlman in Israel, where they filmed some episodes for the US kids' program, *Sesame Street*. One night after filming, the Perlmans invited her to go out with them for dinner. When I picked her up a few hours later at their suite in the Tel Aviv Hilton (and had the honor of meeting not only the Perlmans and their children, but also their friend, Zubin Mehta), I asked her where they'd eaten and she mentioned one of Jaffa's best-known restaurants. On the way home, I asked her if she'd had a steak for dinner. "Are you kidding?" she said, "do you have any idea how expensive that restaurant is — I only ordered a salad." If I needed any justification that I'd done the right thing by raising Rachel in Israel, this was it.

When we left Israel in November 1989, six months after Gadi's death, Rachel auditioned for, and was accepted by, the theater department at the College of Santa Fe. When she came back with me to England that summer for a few months, she had left school with a string of incompletes and was not sure whether or not she'd be going back. Six months later, she'd made the dean's list, was back with her boyfriend Adam, and could not stop talking about the incredible course she was taking on the Holocaust and how she couldn't wait for me to come back to Santa Fe so that I could meet her Holocaust studies teacher. Santa Fe-based medium and psychic Rand Lee once said to me, "I've never met a Jewish person who hasn't had a past life during the Holocaust."

Now in all Israel there was no man so much praised for his beauty as Absalom; from the sole of his foot to the crown of his head there was no blemish on him.

2 Samuel 14:25

It is only with the heart that one can see rightly; what is essential is invisible to the eye.

— Antoine de Saint-Exupéry
The Little Prince

IV
Drops of Magic

Many of us are, today, attuned to our "higher selves" or "guides" or perhaps, as in my case, a highly developed intuition which is always spot-on... whatever we call it, it is our consciousness aligned to our exalted self. And yet, often our fear keeps us separated from our source much of the time, and we therefore utilize so very few of the divine gifts which can open our beings to many of the subtle treasures of spiritual empowerment. The most important thing about these spiritual gifts is that they really help us to be centered and focused. By taking a little time to align with the exalted self and to experience the balance it brings, we support our consciousness by being more together and less fragmented when we go out to deal with a chaotic world. Hypnotherapist and intuitive arts teacher Van R. Ault of San Francisco says that contrary to what many people think, meditation does not need to be unusually formal or elaborate. In fact, he says, the most important things about meditation are that it be simple — straightforward to practice — and that it be practiced regularly.

There are a number of styles of meditation, and it helps to research them and select one that strongly appeals to you. Then, use it diligently — even if it's just opening your heart, inviting your higher power to join you, and sitting silently for five or ten minutes.

Opening your heart and aligning to your exalted self is one of the best ways I know of to eliminate fear. When I listen to the session Gadi had with Miriam, I understand how very frightened he was — particularly of death — and how spiritually lazy he was. Yet, in 1989, even though I sensed Gadi's fears, I certainly couldn't offer him any spiritual advice...I unknowingly still had a great deal of healing to do, a great many fears to overcome.

Linda Goodman writes that "fear is so powerful an emotion, it actually projects a scent or an odor, a most unpleasant one. Animals sense fear in a human or in another animal instantly. Fear, you may not realize, is also a most powerful faith, capable of literally changing the law of physics. *Fear is faith in the negative*, and strong faith manifests its images as swiftly and surely when projected by negative current as by positive."

Gadi, for example, so much wanted to have a million dollars to make his film, but his fears and doubts brought about the opposite, as it always does.

During Gadi's reading with Miriam she said: "You have a very strong desire to do something that will leave its mark — communication is very, very important to you — it's your life-breath. When you're with people you give out signals that you're open, receptive and warm. People who look at you don't know what's inside. Inside is an embarrassed child who often doesn't know what to do or how to feel really good with himself or sure of himself, and sometimes you look in the mirror and you see and feel the polarity, You see two people and only you know which is the person inside and which is the person whom you show to the world... today the focus is stronger and the feeling is that you have to make a drastic change — you feel that you can no longer ignore the situation and the truth is that you don't know what to do about it."

So much of what was said to Gadi at that session felt like a giant verification of many of the things I sensed, but which I'd never discussed with him. I had 'feelings' about many things at that time, but didn't trust my knowing. After Gadi was killed I was haunted by so many questions. And I was angry and in pain. Looking back, I realize that it was the questions, the anger and the pain that created my need to understand, my need to heal. And so I began to read voraciously. Linda Goodman's *Star Signs* opened the gates and I slowly began to comprehend the harmonics of the universe. I came to understand the concept that every experience in our lives occurs to increase our awareness and to bring us closer to God.

Three days after the helicopter crash, the Israeli weekend papers were naturally full of features about Gadi. One article gave this physical description: "tall, with an athletic body, looking at least ten years younger than his age, in jeans and a T-shirt, he always looked so clean — almost innocent — with brown hair bleached by the sun and green eyes. He didn't drink or smoke and when sitting around with the 'boys' during a shoot when they told 'dirty' jokes, he would always laugh like an embarrassed child."

That description took me right back to the first time Gadi and I made love. When I moved to Tel Aviv from Jerusalem, I met Gadi a few times, professionally. Gadi was married and, although I was terribly attracted to him, the idea of a love affair with a married man was not something I entertained.

While I was still living in Jerusalem, soon after I had ended a four-and-a-half-year relationship with Manny, my friend Dhalia came for a visit from the US. Dhalia was born in Israel, but left as a child, and this was her first trip back. I recall how she was so taken by the good-looking men in Israel. Gadi actually looked nothing like the average Israeli hunk, who was typically dark-haired and muscular. Dhalia asked me if perhaps I knew her cousin's husband who was a cinematographer. Small world. I recall telling her that Gadi was the only married man I'd met in Israel that I would have wished to be single. I was actually so happy about the link that, when Dhalia called her cousins to invite them to my flat, I spoke to Gadi on the phone to tell him of the amazing coincidence (the term "synchronicity" was not yet in vogue) of my twenty-year friendship with his wife's cousin. He was thrilled to hear from me and promised to come over with the rest of his family. He never showed up. Years later he told me that he would not have been able to face me in that situation.

When I moved to Tel Aviv I met him for a business lunch and, truly, that's exactly what it was. He was just starting his Election Campaign job. He was a born-and-bred kibbutznick, considered to be left-wing, doing all the visuals for the right-wing Likud party. In Israel the kibbutzim (except for the religious ones), and certainly the artists, theater and film people and the "intelligentsia" are, for the most part, members of the left-wing Labour party. Only after his death did I find out that Gadi's political views were decidedly on the right. It was generally acknowledged that the TV commercial of the Likud party which won them the '86 election was, in fact, Gadi's coup. He found a most engaging little girl and filmed her saying that before the Likud party came to power she had to sleep in a shelter every night because her kibbutz was constantly being shelled by Syria from the Golan Heights. This precious little girl brought the Likud back into the government and gave Israel the intifada, even though it was all a clever PR ploy.

A few days after the elections I received a phone call and didn't recognize his voice. "Who is this?" I asked. "Someone who loves you and your daughter," was the reply. The moments that Gadi would allow himself to be free, open and honest throughout our peripatetic relationship were few, but this was one of them. It never occurred to me that we were about to become lovers. He came over that evening... and an angel came through my door. He was tan, his hair was golden from hundreds of hours filming in the relentless Israeli sun, and he was wearing a white Indian shirt with billowy sleeves — he was just so beautiful — and so very shy. Later, when he came out of the shower, I commented on his incredible body. "Really?" he responded.

"Hasn't anyone ever told you that before?" I asked, very surprised indeed. His "no" was both pleased and embarrassed. Throughout the turbulent years of our relationship he never lost his childlike innocence. He never ceased to be astounded by the fact that sexually he performed more like a 19 year old than the 44 year old he was; he was constantly amazed and proud of himself. To me, a hug is an expression of warmth and caring — to Gadi (and the other Israeli men I had known), a hug was foreplay. I would like to think that in some small way I was instrumental in helping to pave the way for "Hug Therapy" in Israel.

One thing was certain; we embarked on a relationship that was "out of time," and despite Gadi's fears and guilt and the limited amount of time he was able to be with me, whenever we were together the only operative word was *oblivion*. He shyly called our time together "drops of magic". His favorite film was *Blade Runner*, which was directed by Ridley Scott, and he'd seen it seventeen times. When I was living in Santa Fe after leaving Israel, Rachel's roommate brought me an article from *Details* magazine (Nov '90) which was written by Adrian Lyne, the director of *Fatal Attraction*, *9-1/2 Weeks*, and the brilliant but misunderstood *Jacob's Ladder*. The picture she showed me of Adrian Lyne looked exactly like Gadi. It was uncanny. But even more amazing were Lyne's words: "I was hoping to do *Blade Runner*. What Ridley Scott finally did with it was extraordinary, but for me it lacked an element of tragedy — *of falling in love with someone you knew was going to die* [italics mine]." When I read those words it suddenly hit me that, on a soul level I had known that Gadi was going to die. Of course I wasn't conscious of this at the time, but I must admit, looking back, that things about our relationship were totally out of sync with so-called normal relationships.

For instance, I never asked him about his marriage... I somehow always knew that one day he would leave his wife. And, although sometimes weeks would go by between visits, I never felt the need to question him as to his whereabouts. I knew that he was the busiest cinematographer in the country (it was said that he worked every day of the year but Yom Kippur!) and, of course, there was the obligatory 30-day army reserve duty each year and many trips abroad for film work. Whenever he was filming on location in Israel and away from home, I would come and spend a few days with him — I used to tell him jokingly that I was the country's expert on hotel ceilings! Once he was doing a promotional film for a new club hotel in Eilat. Since it was his birthday, I thought that I would go down to Eilat and surprise him. I went to my friend Yossi's Eilat flat and Yossi got him on the phone during a break. "I have a birthday present to deliver to you," said Yossi. "Have a delivery service send it over," said Gadi. "That doesn't seem to be appropriate for this particular present," Yossi said and handed me the phone. "Chamudi, what a wonderful surprise," he said when he heard my voice. "Come over to room 104 at 10 pm." Chamudi was Gadi's pet name for me. It means "sweetie" or "darling".

When I got there, I saw that he had been given a very large suite and thought it quite odd that he would have been given such a large space for only one person, but then I remembered how meagerly Israeli film crews are paid (scriptwriters are among the lowest paid in the world) and just assumed that the hotel had given him a large suite in lieu of payment.

After he died I found out from one "expelled roommate" that there had been another three guys in the suite and that Gadi had somehow managed to get them to leave. Lord knows what he told them, but that night in Eilat was undoubtedly the most magical night we ever spent together. Those drops of magic became a flood! The next day I enjoyed the facilities of the club and lounged by the pool pretending not to know him while he and his Steadicam were just a few feet away. Unfortunately, the only flight I could get a seat on back to Tel Aviv was his flight, which was, on the other hand, lucky because I had left my silk Chinese robe in his suite. There was a sticky moment at the airport when we simultaneously opened our respective suitcases and he slipped me the robe. The Arkia flight was delayed and in the waiting room he introduced me to the producer and his wife (as a friend who just happened to be there). Aviva and I subsequently became friends and she later told me that the entire day's filming had to be redone, that Gadi had shot unusable footage because "he had taken up with an eighteen-year-old kid and obviously couldn't, after spending the night with her, see properly."

Although I firmly believe that we choose our lives and our karmic scripts, I have also come to realize that people who are controlled by the subconscious machinations of fear, as Gadi certainly was, must start to make decisions out of love if they are to survive. If this is improperly understood, as by those who comprehend fragments and not the wholeness of what is occurring on the planet today, and by those people whose minds do not function in tandem with their hearts, the coming changes do indeed have the potential to inspire fear. Shirley MacLaine, in her book *Dance While You Can*, says that being on a spiritual path without first working through healing and forgiveness within our immediate families is valueless. Although I had always felt that Gadi would eventually leave his wife, I was nonetheless almost knocked over when, during the session with Miriam, he said: "The big moment has arrived — my wife. Today we are in total breakdown... total... total... total... and if you want me to focus on a question I'll ask if there is any future despite the fact that we try to work it out and get hurt, only to try again and again to be hurt even more."

Everything I'd sensed about Gadi's marriage was why I'd continued to see him. Now I was hearing the very words he'd never shared with me.

And then, at the very end of the session, he asked: "Can you tell me... this is not a fair question... if she is seeing anyone else... not that I care."

Miriam said, "It's not a fair question."

Gadi again said, "Not that I care," and I was thinking, fair or not fair, let's have an answer. Four years of my life had been bound up with this man... I had known more pain (and more joy) than I was sometimes able to bear, and dammit, if Gadi wanted to know if there was another man in his wife's life — and asked it in my presence — this was one answer I had to hear!

Again Miriam responded with, "It's not a fair question."

"If I cared, I wouldn't have asked. I just want to know," said Gadi.

And Miriam answered, "Very possibly yes."

"C'est tout," said Gadi.

And when Saul saw the army of the Philistines, he was
afraid, and his heart greatly trembled. And when Saul
inquired of the Lord, he did not answer him, either by
dreams or by fire or by prophets.

1 Samuel 5:6

But on your tiny planet, my little prince, all you need
to do is move your chair a few steps. You can see the
day end and the twilight falling whenever you like...
"One day," you said to me, "I saw the sunset forty-four
times!"

— Antoine d' Saint-Exupéry
The Little Prince

V

Conflicts of Spirit

During the last months of his life, something subtle had changed within our relationship. Not that Gadi had lost his fears, but he seemed somehow more relaxed. He started spending more time with me, often doing some editing work or preparing for the next day's filming. He was no longer living at home, but this was something I didn't find out until after his death, as well as other "secrets" he kept from me. During the reading, Miriam had said to him, "You have much potential creativity — the ability to express yourself — to connect people and things. These things can help you in alleviating your fears. Today, your ability to face these things is much greater, and the feeling that you can is today much stronger. It's not enough, but it's a beginning — you're always moving from place to place, from person to person, from conversation to conversation; distant places, nature — these things really excite you."

At that point Miriam invited Gadi to ask questions, to which he replied, "What can I ask? What does one ask?"

Miriam answered him with: "You can relate to what was said, you can ask for explanations, things that hurt or bother you, or you can touch the point of fear and open it up and understand why and from where it is happening. You can ask about relationships — any relationship — but you must ask from your heart and not from your head."

Gadi then said, "It's important for me to know where I stand in relationship to the others in my profession, where I'll be in a few years, and if I'll be successful. Success for me is to rest in peace on some island in Tahiti and enjoy life, and only money can bring me there. Is my purpose, my strength, my power known? If it were known, I would have greater motivation than I do now, because I believe in myself — but on the other hand, I don't believe in myself because I know that Israeli society with its boundaries and limitations, the Arabs — everything brings it down–and I'm not smart enough or talented enough to make changes in my life."

Miriam's response came through the heart to someone who was obviously so full of fears that only his head heard the words: "You make more of yourself and you belittle yourself. There are places where you are stuck and fears which prevent you from forging ahead. You were told in the beginning that you have to cross over that stumbling block that's stopping you and then you can really go on your own power and strength — the inner strength, not the external — because until you can really open your heart, until you can truly see that success comes the moment you feel that you are manifesting your heart's desire, then everything falls into place and happens. The bottom line is that everything has to come from within you. When it comes from within with total belief and complete faith, then nothing can stop you or block you. Right now the contact with the spirit guides — at least one specific guide — is on a very high level of awareness and knowledge: they can read you from top to bottom like an open book. But because they can 'see,' they know exactly how much at this moment you are willing to open your heart, but the fears are yours and only you can ask. It's not proper that they bring them up because they won't give you what you aren't ready to receive. However, you have the opportunity to ask exactly what you want, and you will get the answers that will truly open everything up."

"So what does a person ask at such an encounter?" Gadi queried. "OK, he gets some reinforcement about things he more or less knows — that he has to bring things out in the open, to believe in what he wants or he won't succeed; he knows that he's sensitive, talented, that he knows how to love, how to be unfaithful — he knows all those things — so why is he obsessed constantly with the million dollars waiting for him in a briefcase on Dizengoff Street? Why? Because all the paths are blocked? So why? Because his great talent is hampered by his shyness and insecurities?"

"No, no road is blocked, but you're stuck by thinking that the million dollars is the answer," said Miriam. "If you had to choose between the million dollars and the things you love, it's fair to say that you would choose the things you love, and not the million dollars. Your choice."

To which Gadi predictably replied, "I'm ready to take the million dollars and continue to stay with the things I love, because the financial gain will help me succeed, won't it?"

"You place too much importance on what people think of you. It's not important what others think of you — only that you love yourself. You constantly feel that you have to reach a certain standard, as if your life is a competition. In actuality, life isn't a competition. You can go step by step on your path and reach your destination, and then you have really gotten there on your own power — and then the others get there, too — but at that point it doesn't make any difference. This is a very significant point. You can spend your whole life looking for the million dollars on every corner; you might never find it and you might never be happy because you'll always feel that something is missing because you're going on the material — you're making the material the objective. The moment you put the inner-you first — and go with your heart — you can't lose. Believe me, this is not meaningless talk."

Louise Hay, author of *Heal Your Body* and *You Can Heal Your Life*, says that true prosperity begins with feeling good about ourselves; that is the freedom to do what we want to do, when we want to do it. Our own belief in lack and limitation is the only thing that is limiting us. For twenty-six years, I believed that I had been responsible for the death of my infant brother, and of course it followed that if I had done such a terrible thing, then I was not worthy of prosperity. According to Hay, the use of affirmations helps us look at our lives in a different way, and the more we begin to trust the process of life, the more life flows for us. About a year ago, I began to use the affirmation "I am a magnet for divine prosperity" and couldn't understand why money wasn't coming to me. Mind you, other things were coming to me; I was meeting the most extraordinarily evolved people, and miracles were manifesting in my life. Then I realized that what I was receiving was divine prosperity — exactly what I'd been asking for! I then changed the affirmation to "I am open and receiving lavish goodness from all directions of God," and within a week I received, totally unexpectedly, a check for $400! I have come to trust the process of life–to go with the flow–and have found that the more I trust, the more life flows for me.

Gadi's spiritual-material conflict was made clear to me when, toward the end of the session with Miriam he said, " I'm lost because I can't succeed — I'm in such a cage. I have a terrible premonition about what's going to happen here — and it traps us all, and I resent it so much — that I feel that I have to be a fatalist and remain when everything falls. I have a tremendous fear even to say what's going to happen here. I wrote a script for my daughter and suddenly I realized that I'm writing a script for my daughter's cinema class entitled 'The Final Days of the State of Israel' — I believe completely that this is what's going to happen. That's the trap that ensnares me, and that's why I'm lost. When we started sitting here, I asked myself, "What shall I write as a heading for what she is going to tell me? — maybe she'll tell it like it is, maybe not. Who is she anyway? and — my hand wrote by itself — do you see what it wrote — 'A Passing Breeze' — just like that. I didn't know what I was writing, but suddenly I saw myself — I'm in the desert... it's unbearably hot... no water... we won't find any solution–but at least she'll bring me a cool breeze." He was, of course, referring to Miriam. Then he said, "I don't believe in Sunny and everything she tells me. I don't believe one word she says. All these years with fortune tellers she scrambles my brain."

Turning to me for a moment, he said, "What are you getting upset for? I don't believe in anything she says because she is more mistaken than all the people in the world, so why should I believe her?"

And truly I had no answer to give him. I was just starting out on my own spiritual journey and had many more questions than answers.

"But I came here open," he continued. "My soul will go out the window, it'll go out the window. My soul will stay on the chair, it'll stay on the chair. Nothing will shock me — suddenly I feel that there's no death but, since there's nothing else, then there is death. I remember reading about a monk who lived five hundred years ago and spoke about death — he called it 'drops of magic.' As he said that he winked at me. "There's no chance that I'll remember the name of this monk, because I'm a real degenerate in these things, a name that goes round and round. Something like Figorella, I don't remember, but the name goes round and round."

Miriam added, "You know, I got this picture: You're in an upside-down forest and you're running and running and trying to catch a ball that's going round. The entire solution is just to grab it, go for it. But you don't see the ball; you can catch it, you can grab it; it's not so round."

And Gadi responded with, "I can?"

Miriam continued, "You perceive it totally in another shape…if you could just see the shape, just grasp it…that's what I saw, a real picture; but everything is upside down."

For thy heavens have seen the work of thy fingers, the moon and the stars, which thou hast ordained. What is man, that thou art mindful of him? and the son of man, that thou visitest him?

For thou hast made him a little lower than the angels, and hast clothed him in glory and honor.

Psalm 8: 3-5

VI

Opening to Spirit

ב When I said earlier that on a soul level I knew Gadi was going to die or even that, by the very tone and resonance of the questions and statements he made during his session with Miriam, the soul knew that its days in Gadi's magnificent body were numbered, truly neither of us had any idea of what was to come. After the reading, Miriam called me up and said that, looking at Gadi's astrological chart, she saw danger in flying over the following two weeks. Gadi assured me that he wouldn't be leaving for the Philippines for two weeks (and Miriam obviously wasn't going to check out his chart for the next two months). Of his experience flying in the Congo during a lightning storm, he had said, "I wasn't frightened even for one second... 'OK', I said, 'we'll die, so we'll die.' Something that doesn't happen to me on the ground. I'm telling you all of this so that you'll start taking me seriously."

And Miriam replied, "They're guarding you — they watch over you with the big things... the small things you have to take care of yourself. There are periods, times when you have to be really careful, aware and pay attention." At the end of the session, Gadi asked Miriam if he were to give her the name of someone, would she be able to give him some information about that person? She said that she could, but she would leave it for another time. Gadi then gave her the name of a woman whom he said he'd met in Kenya. I must say that as soon as I heard her name I got a really weird feeling, but gave the matter no further thought.

Our intuition is always spot-on about these things... sometimes, if you ask people who claim to have no interest whatsoever in spiritual matters if they've ever felt an instant dislike for someone, they will invariably tell you that they have. My friend Melanie says that both the instant "like" and "dislike" that people experience is their awareness of another person's vibrations. A feeling of distrust with no apparent foundation, which subsequently proves to be correct, can often make a case for reincarnation to even the most skeptical person.

Anyway, the night that Gadi was to leave for what was meant to be two weeks to film a documentary in the Philippines, Miriam phoned me somewhat distraught. She had received information on the name of the woman Gadi had asked her about, and he had promised to call her before his flight. At midnight, she hadn't yet heard from him. She had just read the transmitted information (I could easily relate to that: when I read back my automatic writing I often don't recognize it, or feel that I am reading something for the first time) and felt that it was important that Gadi hear it before he left. She then read it to me. It was in extremely literary and flowery Hebrew — I only understood about 80% of it, enough to pick up that there had been something sexual between them which, if the connection between them continued, would have dire consequences. There was a physical description of the woman, and when Miriam read it to me, I kept thinking, "He slept with this woman in Kenya a few months ago — Kenya, for God's sake, one of the countries with the highest number of AIDS cases — and he didn't even tell me about it and here we've been having unprotected sex for months." I left a message at the airport for Gadi to call both Miriam and me before leaving the country. When he called me from a phone box he told me he had only one token and could I call him back.

It was so typical. In the nine years I'd known him, the only thing he'd ever given me was a black kitten when his cat had a litter in 1985. We used to live about 30 minutes apart and whenever he had some free time he would call me and I would drive the half hour to pick him up. Once I stopped at a delicatessen to buy some hummus and salads. Next door was a pita bakery. I think that six pitas cost something like 25¢. I asked him if he would run in and pick up half-a-dozen pitas, and he said, "Give me some money. I'm broke."

So it wasn't the phone token which upset me, it wasn't even the fact that he'd slept with someone on location (a film industry hazard); it was the fact that he had always told me that actors were the lowest of the low and, as it turned out when I phoned him back, she had been an actress and "somebody had given him something lethal to smoke and the next thing he knew etc. etc."

"Would you please go and get tested for AIDS in Manila?" I asked.

"No," he answered, "you go and get tested." (Somehow there was a flashback to my marriage here. When I said to my husband that the only way I would agree not to file for divorce would be if he would go for some counseling, he responded with: "I don't need counseling; you need counseling.")

He was interested in the information Miriam had received and asked me to fax it to him in Manila. He did say that he was not interested in this woman from Kenya, that she was very persistent but that it had only been a "one night stand" and that he would be back in Israel in two weeks and we would talk about him moving in with me and Rachel when he came back.

With Miriam's reading I also faxed him a letter telling him I had just seen the film *The Accidental Tourist* and was very taken by the line spoken by William Hurt when he says: "You know, I've come to realize that it's not how much you love someone, but how you are when you're with that person that is important." I wrote that I hoped he would have time to listen to the tapes from the session with Miriam, and that I couldn't understand how he could keep from me and, more importantly, from his wife, this "accidental liaison" in Kenya, and that I was going to have a blood test, that I thought he was super-irresponsible, and that I hoped he would have some time to work out his problems. I sent the letters from a mutual friend's production office facsimile machine.

Gadi didn't come back after two weeks; he hadn't called me after I sent him the letter. This was, incidentally, the very first time in all the years that I had known him that I had actually complained about the way he treated me. In the meantime, I went for a blood test, tested HIV-negative, and tried to get hold of Gadi in Manila. When I heard his voice, the line suddenly went dead. I had the operator place the call for me a second time. This time Gadi spoke to me. "What happened a minute ago?" I asked.

"I hung up on you," he replied.

"What on earth for?"

"Because you're sending faxes through Ben's office — my wife is very friendly with him, that's why! And all the world can read your letters." The truth is, I had gone to Ben's office to send the fax myself. Never in a million years would I have shared that fax with anybody. After all, hadn't I recently found that Gadi's marriage was over, and hadn't Gadi all but promised me that he would be moving in with me? After so many years of playing games, it seemed that finally things were coming together, but I knew what a small country Israel is and how Gadi could be so terribly paranoid. I used to say that if you sneezed in Tel Aviv someone would say "Gezhundheit" in Jerusalem.

As mentioned, Gadi's name came to the compound number 12, "The Sacrifice; the Victim," and the reading in *Star Sign* starts with: "One will periodically be sacrificed for the plans or intrigues of others. The number 12 warns of the necessity to be alert to every situation, to beware of false flattery from those who use it to gain their own ends. Be suspicious of those who offer a high position, and carefully analyze the motive.... " I later found out that while in the Philippines he was offered the position as second unit cameraman on the production of *Delta Force II*, and the promise of some very good money was just too much for him to resist. I did the numerology of my name also, and I nearly fainted at the accuracy — I was reading the story of my life. It said: "26/ Partnerships: This compound number vibrates, in a strange way to a unique kind of power, based on compassion and unselfishness, with the ability to help others but not always the self. It warns of dangers, disappointments, and failure, especially regarding the ambitions, brought about through bad advice, associations with others and unhappy partnerships of all kinds." (I subsequently did change the spelling of my name, and cannot begin to describe the tremendous difference it has made in my life.)

The day after the accident, Miriam phoned me up and said that she felt that Gadi wanted to communicate, and may she come over. My friends Robin and Judi were with me. I had been up most of the night and was, I believe, still uncomprehending. Nearly seven weeks had gone by since he'd left Israel. I wasn't happy about the woman from Kenya, there were so many things I felt I'd never be able to talk to Gadi about, so many things left unsaid. I'd given this man unconditional love and all I felt — the day after his death–was a tremendous sense of betrayal. Reading *Star Signs* while Gadi was away had had a tremendous effect on me and I felt, for the first time, that I would have been able to explain many things to Gadi which had come out during the session with Miriam which, two months earlier, I hadn't understood. So I was feeling cheated — and angry. Now I'd finally come to understand that we each can choose to govern and ordain our personal destinies — that we each can be the master of our own fate. Intellectually I knew that death was not the end, but my heart was broken… and even if death wasn't the end, how could I ever continue to have a "relationship" with Gadi? So when Miriam sat opposite me in my living room, I told Judi and Robin that I thought the whole thing was bullshit. Miriam started by telling me that I was covered in light. "I can hardly look at you because the light is so bright," she said.

Then her voice changed, and she started to speak very slowly, as if each word was a supreme effort. Gadi was speaking through her! "I'm in a strange place… I can see you… but I can't touch. Everything is upside down… I want to return… it's as if I haven't seen you for a year." For some reason I knew that this was real, and I suddenly felt that I was really speaking to Gadi and I asked him, "What happened?" as if indeed he was in the room with me.

"Don't know… wasn't frightened… love to fly… feel at home… I never told you how much I love you… even from afar. I know how much you love me … didn't show my love like you… but I want you to know that I love you very much… don't forget our times of togetherness … our drops of magic… and your desire to succeed. Don't forget me. Tell my children not to be angry with me and not to forget me. Tell my wife not to be angry about the breakdown during this last period…."

Gadi once told me that if his wife found out about us "she would kill me." I doubt that that would have happened, but his messages to his wife and children were for me genuine proof that Gadi was communicating from "the other side." Miriam knew very little about our relationship, and so the words "drops of magic" could only have been Gadi's and, most importantly, he never told me how much he loved me when he was alive and that was something only he and I knew. At that point I truly felt that he was with me in the living room, and I spoke to him with an ease and a naturalness I hadn't believed was possible. "You're on the front pages of the newspapers and on TV," I said.

"Well, at least it's publicity. I love to talk… I have a lot to say… I want to talk, but now I think I have to go. Miriam's friends are helping me… I love her very much… I love you very much…." So, the contact which had been made with Miriam's spirit guides during the session in March was actually helping Gadi make his transition! (In *Ghost*, less than a year later, Demi Moore would single handedly persuade a young generation of cynics in 127 minutes that love can indeed conquer death — while simultaneously netting Paramount Pictures a cool $203 million.) Gadi spoke through Miriam for all of five minutes, yet I suddenly felt tremendously blessed that I was to be part of something that was divinely ordained — and not at all sad. Gadi had made his soul choice… he was going to help from the other side! I understood this with my head immediately, but it would take my heart much longer to absorb this spiritual bond he was creating with me.

The very next day, all the weekend papers ran full-page articles about Gadi. The headline of one paper ran HIS INCREDIBLE RELATIONSHIP WITH LIGHT. HIS GREAT LOVE OF SUNSETS. The article said that he was the country's leading expert on light. That he loved Israel, not as an idealist, but with an instinct which defied the rules… "he knew this country so well that it was as if the map of Israel had been emblazoned on his forehead." The exact details of the crash were sketchy, and only six months later, with the December '89 issue of *Premiere Magazine*, would I learn that of the five killed, only Gadi died instantly.

"Those who reached the site worked heroically to free the victims. Schultz lifted the side of the chopper while Solo pulled out Gadi Danzig's body. 'I knew he was dead,' says Solo. 'I reached around him and his chest felt like a bag of popcorn. I just said, God bless you Gadi.(*Premier Magazine* p.110) "Death in the Philippines" Nov. 1989)

My cousin Pippa (who'd "seen" Miriam's spirit guides) described a psychic picture she'd seen of how the helicopter fell and crashed (which was graphically confirmed — exactly as she described it — months later when I saw a film clip of the accident on the TV program *Entertainment Tonight*), and claimed that Gadi was filming and standing up as the chopper went down; that he was not strapped in; and that on impact the camera lens went right through his forehead (or, to put it spiritually, instantaneously opened up his third eye).

The article in the Hebrew paper continued:

"Sunsets — he was absolutely enamored of them. Sometimes he would stop filming in the middle of something and turn his camera toward the setting sun and say: 'This isn't your business... this shot isn't for this film; it's for me.' Once I saw him standing and filming the wall... I couldn't understand what he was doing until I realized that hanging on that wall was a picture of a sunset!"

When I read this, I was reminded of my favorite book of all time, Saint Exupéry's magical *The Little Prince*, particularly the parts about sunsets.

A few days after the accident, it hit me that among Gadi's personal effects would be the tapes from his session with Miriam, and I thought it best that they not get to his wife for the time being. I managed to find out which of his friends was arranging to have his body flown from the Philippines to Israel for the funeral. When the time was right, I explained, I would get a set of the tapes to Gadi's parents and to his eldest child, his son. Gadi had actually left them a message on the tapes, and I knew that I was meant to be the "messenger" — it's just that the time was inappropriate. This friend promised me that he would be certain to do as I asked. He didn't. A few months later, when I made contact with Gadi's kid brother, he told me that he had heard that there were some tapes with important messages from Gadi, which he and his family would very much like to have a copy of, but Gadi's wife, with the only copy, was not willing to share them with his family on the kibbutz. I immediately sent copies off to him, as I was about to leave Israel at that point, and I knew that was what Gadi would have wanted.

How beautiful are your breasts, O my sister, my bride! how much better are your breasts than wine! and the fragrance of your ointments than all spices!

Song of Solomon 4:10

VII

Feline Spirit

Since his "death" four weeks earlier, I had had two "contacts" with Gadi — the one through Miriam the day after the helicopter crash, and another very weird occurrence eight days later.

On that particular evening I met my friend Tova, who was up from Jerusalem, at a restaurant. Tova and I had been friends for years. I lovingly called her a JIP — a term I coined for a "Jewish-Israeli Princess." During dinner I commented that even though the way Gadi had spoken to me — through Miriam — was intellectually tempting to take at face value, it was still too soon and my grief too fresh (and my understanding of the spiritual realm too limited) for me to truly believe that Gadi actually had "come through" Miriam. Plus the fact that Miriam had met Gadi. "If he'd come through my cat," I jokingly said to Tova, "then I'd be more convinced."

Gadi and I shared a love of cats. When I moved to Tel Aviv, his black and white cat, Copy, had just had a litter, so Rachel and I took a kitten whom we called Sheba. A few months before Gadi was killed, Copy had died and Gadi was shattered. Returning home after dinner with Tova, I was thinking that I had read somewhere that it takes the soul nine days to find its peace.

As I walked up the stairs to my second-floor flat, I thought that I felt Gadi's presence, but dismissed it as wishful thinking. I recall that I was wearing jeans and a T-shirt. I came into my bedroom, removed my bra and T-shirt, but not my jeans, and lay on my bed — half dressed — reading Linda Goodman's *Star Signs*. Strangely, I still felt a presence in the room.

Lounging around topless was not something I normally did. Gadi had never been a great one for compliments. His eyes usually said more than his mouth. I sometimes felt that he was swallowing all the things he wanted to say to me but couldn't. So naturally I remembered the exact words (and place and time) of the few compliments he doled out. Once he looked at me and said, "You're so beautiful," and I felt that those three words were the most genuine and heartfelt words that any man had ever said to me. Compliment number two went like this: "You have the most tempting breasts in 1) the whole world, 2) the entire Middle East."

This one was harder for me to deal with. I'd always been what they call in England "a bonnie lass" or in Philadelphia, "zoftik," at least in the Jewish neighborhoods. Back in 1969, my husband-to-be and I had spent a week looking for a wedding dress. Uri knew no English back then, but after the first grueling shopping day, he told me he'd learned his first word in English — "busty." When people would ask me why I stayed in Israel for so long, I'd say that the whole country's male population liked "zoftik" women.

So there I was, 38DD, sitting and reading, when I said out loud, "Eat your heart out, you bastard," and all of a sudden my cat, Pumpkin, jumped up on the bed and started behaving... in a way that cats simply do not behave. He started touching me with his mouth, very gently all over my ears, neck, shoulders and breasts. Like it was Gadi. But I've had cats all my life and I can say, unequivocally, this was definitely otherworldly! It lasted for about five minutes and it probably was the strangest encounter I'd ever experienced. That small, instinctual voice inside told me that I should take a shower, light a candle, play our favorite U2 tape, *Joshua Tree*... that is, create the correct ambience (after all, I had been educated by *Cosmopolitan* every month since I was 16). I got up to go to take a shower. Pumpkin stayed on the bed. It was the first time in four years that he did not follow me, hoping (as always hope springs eternal in the feline heart) that I would be detouring through the kitchen. It was almost as if Gadi was waiting for me in bed while I went about my toilette. I was almost tempted to bring a plate of chocolate chip cookies back to the bedroom with me. However, by the time I'd showered, dimmed the lights, lit a candle and had *Joshua Tree* on the stereo, Pumpkin had gone back to being his usual Garfield-like self and was checking out his dinner menu.

Within eight days of each other I'd had two contacts with Gadi, so to speak, and my limited knowledge of these things nonetheless did seem to point to the fact that he was trying to communicate with me, tell me that his personality had not died and, I thought to tell me that he loved me.

About a week after the article appeared, Miriam came over to see me. She was, I hoped, going to tell me that her phone had been ringing off the hook and that she was booked for sessions for the next twelve months. But no, she had to see me face-to-face because she had some very distressing news for me. My distress-level was so high it was off the scale, so I couldn't imagine what she could possibly tell me that would distress me any more. That's when I learned of Gadi's live-in lover. The woman called and then came to Miriam, totally at her wits' end and speaking of suicide.

As hurt, angry and confused as I was, I felt that I should meet with this person. Not to "check her out" or anything, but to try to come to terms with this bolt out of the blue. According to Miriam, they had had a very serious relationship. Something was not right. Gadi, especially during his last months with me, had changed. He was less fearful of "being found out" and had begun to spend more quality time with me, and was much more comfortable in his relationship with Rachel. I actually thought that, even though I was still a bit confused about this "death" thing, I could at least tell her about what occurred the day after he died and the cat incident. But Miriam said that Rinat was definitely not interested in meeting me. Miriam had spent hours with her and was clearly convinced that Gadi's relationship with Rinat was "the real thing", whilst what he had shared with me for four years was pure lust. This was not Miriam, the transchannel speaking; no, this was after speaking with Rinat woman-to-woman.

Now I must say that Miriam knew very few details about my situation with Gadi. He was, after all, married and very well-known in Israel, and discretion was very important to him (that's what he called it when he was alive; I've since come to understand that his whole life was based in fear). Fear, as I mentioned earlier, is faith in the negative, or, an acronym for *False Evidence Appears Real.* He was often afraid that I would tell the world about our affair. When we are in conflict internally, our lives are marked by external conflicts. And I have seen that, amazingly, when we finally resolve our internal conflicts, the outer ones just seem to melt away. In Gadi's case, it slowly became apparent that he was able to resolve his inner conflicts only from the "other side."

I began to think about the nine months prior to his "death." I went back to August and September of '88. In August Gadi spent the month doing his yearly thirty-day army reserve stint. I was waiting for a flat to be ready in Tel Aviv, my prior lease had ended, and I was living temporarily in an apartment hotel, not far from the area that Gadi and I both had called home. Rachel was visiting her grandparents in England, and I remember missing Gadi terribly throughout that entire month. I even sent him a letter care of the army, which he never received and, when I told him of it, he was very angry because it could have been sent to his home where his wife would have opened it. He said that things were not good at home, but I didn't press him for details. Soon after, he started to work exclusively through a pager service, and I rarely called him at home from that point. During the nine months, he spent a couple of months in Kenya, somewhere else out of Israel for at least another month, seven weeks in the Philippines, and a month doing his Army Reserve duty, so this nine-month relationship with Rinat was already dwindled down to three months.

I tried calling Rinat, but she refused to speak with me. I was in a constant state of bewilderment. On the one hand, after four years of a roller-coaster love affair, I had genuinely felt that the last four months with Gadi were finally looking like a relationship that seemed to have definite future possibilities; on the other hand, he had been living apart from his wife and family and with another woman, and had shared none of this with me. Miriam told me that Rinat and Gadi were madly in love, and I kept asking myself why he didn't just come to me and tell me he had fallen in love with someone else. It would have hurt, but I would have preferred the honesty.

I had so many things that I wanted to talk to Gadi about. Little did

I know that in the not-too-distant future Gadi would have the ability to communicate directly with me and explain everything he was never able to talk about when he was alive.

Truly light is sweet, and it is a pleasant thing for the eyes; but much more to those who see the sun.*

Ecclesiastes 11:7

* Sun is often used symbolically meaning the truth.
Light symbols enlightenment.
God is often spoken of as Sun.

VIII

Beacon of Light

Everything was falling apart in my world. Gadi was gone, leaving a wife, three children, parents, a brother and sister, and at least two women who had each been convinced that she was "the other woman." The funeral took place well over a week after the crash — there were some serious weather conditions in the Philippines, and it took days before they were able to fly his body home.

I had this crazy desire to buy something new and colorful for the funeral. I'd never been to a funeral in Israel, and I felt that Gadi wouldn't have wanted me to be in black — I didn't remember ever seeing him dressed in black. In a boutique around the corner from my flat, I found a wonderful skirt of purple, blue, magenta, and red, a potpourri of dancing colors that I wore with a red silk blouse. Gadi's friends — those who had promised to remove the "Miriam tapes" from Gadi's things– "suggested" to me that I maintain a very low profile at the funeral. Instead, I was a swishing rainbow of primary colors.

Since Gadi "passed over" in 1989, I have been on a spiritual search which has yielded much fruit. Perhaps the golden apple belongs to the work being done by the Aquarius Spiritual Education Center in Kansas City, Missouri, particularly their studies on Vibrational Recognition and Harmony. The operative principle here is that "no thing, no life form, no condition, no event is without vibration." "Red is the most powerful color of one's lower nature," they say. "It automatically invokes an intense response, for it is intense. It is the color of fire; emotional fires are ignited. Subconsciously or consciously everyone responds to red in some manner. Red invites response."

So here I was at Gadi's funeral, where I had been asked to keep a low profile, wearing a bright red blouse! There were hundreds of people there and, as it took place on his kibbutz, mostly everybody was dressed very casually, with jeans being quite prominent, but I don't recall seeing anyone in black.

Black, according to the Aquarian Life Lessons, has only the qualities of passive void. Black is not a color; it is the lack of all light, the lack of all life. It is deadness. It is only in combination with red that it has any powerful action, and then its only action is negative. The Aquarian Life Lessons home study program states that "you are capable of knowing intuitively what you do not have as intellectual knowledge." And then they pose the question, what color is war? And what color is violence? They say that most of us answer "red" and "black" and claim that our answer comes from an intuitive "knowing." Because the majority of mankind has no knowledge of the real significance and powers of color, red and black are constantly used in combination which, they believe, causes many disturbing conditions within the health and affairs of mankind, but, more importantly,

"it is perpetuating crime, violence and wars. Imagine that all of the items in this combination of color are constantly attuning the Earth and her inhabitants to the terrible violence already existing. This automatically gives these conditions more power. We are not making suppositions here. We are telling you a truth. It is a Universal Law of Magnetism that like attracts like. Do not doubt it. Begin to recognize these powers of color and attune yourself accordingly."

So I chose to get rid of all my clothing which was either red, black or a combination of both, because I did understand that "the colors of clothing have the most power to affect you personally since they are actually worn upon the body" and that if I am seeking enlightenment and greater alignment with the soul, it makes sense to consider my wardrobe. I have come to see that if we stay within the Laws of God, we will automatically attain our spiritual goals, and that it cannot be otherwise, for it is Universal Law.

It was at this time, while I was living in London, that the Prince and Princess of Wales announced their separation. The following day, the

Evening Standard ran a picture of Diana on the front page. She was dressed in black and looked positively glum. Inside on page three was a picture of Prince Charles sitting in a car with his PR "girl" (as the UK press called her). She was wearing red and black and looked really angry, and Prince Charles was wearing a navy blue suit and a light blue shirt and was actually smiling. All shades of blue, from the lightest to the very darkest, are extremely healthful for all individuals, according to the Aquarian Life Lessons, and it's the pastel colors which are vibrationally high and help us to raise our personal vibrations more quickly.

There were hundreds of people at the kibbutz that bright and sunny May day. The kibbutz was alive with the vibrant colors of spring, and Gadi was buried under what had been his favorite spot when he was growing up there. Everyone stood in line and put stones on the mound of fresh earth. When my turn came up, I suddenly put my hand in my pocket and took out my quartz crystal and buried it in the soil. An impulse.

A few months earlier, when I had given Gadi the channeled message from Miriam, I had also given him a quartz crystal as a birthday present. Right before he went to the Philippines, I asked him over the phone if he had the crystal on him, and he said he did. "Keep it with you at all times," I remember saying to him. "It will protect you." My crystal was part of the same cluster as the one I had given Gadi, so it somehow seemed appropriate to return it to the earth where Gadi's body lay — a body that still haunts me. Right before I left Israel I asked Rinat if she remembered the crystal. She did. Gadi gave to her right after I'd given it to him. He never even took it with him. I wonder, if he had, would it have protected him?

Around the time I took Gadi to Miriam's, I was interviewed by a Tel Aviv newspaper regarding a feature film I was desperately trying to produce, and Rachel asked me not to do the interview. "I just don't have a good feeling about this, Mom," she said to me. The truth is that Rachel's intuitions were always "spot on." The two-page spread about my film appeared with the 36-point headline: "Hollywood Here She Comes." Rachel was not impressed. Nor, for that matter, was Gadi.

"This country eats you alive," he said. "You're so incredibly talented, go to California where you'll be appreciated. If I wasn't so damned scared and reluctant to leave my kids, I'd be there in a flash."

But at that point, when I believed that Gadi was moments away from leaving his wife, and Rachel was preparing for her matriculation exams in her last year of high school, I wasn't going anywhere.

The film I was working on was a holocaust black comedy based on a book that was, and is, considered one of the best stories ever written in Israel. It's called *To Remember, to Forget* and the author, Dahn Ben Amotz, was easily the "enfant terrible" and the "bête noire" of Israel, bar none. The first time I went to see him regarding the rights (the book was 20 years old), in the middle of the conversation he walked into his bathroom, which was right in front of where I was sitting, and urinated in front of me! The Israelis "in the know" (actually, that means every single Israeli in the country) told me that if I wanted to buy the rights from him, I should send my daughter, as he had a reputation not unlike that of Roman Polanski, albeit on a smaller scale.

The story of *To Remember, to Forget* had emblazoned itself on my soul — a 29-year-old Israeli man, born in Germany, goes back there in 1959 to collect reparation money and meets and falls in love with a young German woman. How he deals with his guilt (mostly by denial) when his new bride drives him to Dachau on their honeymoon, and how he appears at the social event of the year — the Frankfurt costume ball — as a Hasidic Jew, are some of the most hysterical, yet poignant scenes I had ever read, and I spent over a year trying to get this project off the ground.

Rachel had first brought the book to my attention. She was reading it after hearing a talk from a holocaust survivor in school and was so moved that she went up to him and hugged him after the talk. The man actually called me up and said, "I've been speaking in schools all over Israel for many years — hundreds of schools, thousands of kids — yet I've never met a soul like your daughter's, and I just had to call and tell you how very special she is and how I hope that she will read as much on the subject as possible." When I asked what she was in fact reading, she showed me Ben Amotz's book in Hebrew. And then she said, "You have this book in English up there on the top shelf of the bookcase."

Now this was the weirdest thing. I knew my books, knew them very well, in fact. My library was very dear to me, and when I went to live abroad I had to choose very carefully because I wasn't able to take most of them. Since my degree was in English literature, I had acquired hundreds of books over the university and ensuing years and had really only brought those which I thought "I couldn't live without." It's amazing, in retrospect, as my current library does not contain any of those books today, except Saint Exupéry's *The Little Prince*. So where could this English translation of *To Remember, to Forget* come from? (Probably, I realized, from Philadelphia when I had worked as Marketing Director of the Jewish Publication Society.) I had taken a few titles with me, although until that moment I never realized that I had that particular book. So Rachel and I shared a literary experience which was profound for both of us. Seven years later Tom Robbins's *Jitterbug Perfume* and his *Skinny Legs and All* would unite our souls even more powerfully.

I was driven by this book and hoped that the article about my attempts to get a film produced would manifest an angel who would purchase the rights. I was too dense to see the negative energy that surrounded this project. Soon after the article appeared, Ben Amotz was diagnosed with liver cancer. He held a big party for all his friends in Tel Aviv, and the papers had a field day. He was dying and intending to leave in a manner that no one in Israel would forget. I called him and asked him if he would mind if a healer friend visited him. He screamed at me, told me he had plenty of friends and didn't need any assistance from me. I also wanted to change the title from *To Remember, to Forget* to "To Remember, to Forgive", but he was having none of my "spiritual shit," and then the nonspiritual shit really hit the fan. After months of negotiating with a German producer, I put together a co-production between the Israelis and the Germans and, because I believed so much in Gadi's talent, I wanted him to direct it.

I'd had the opportunity to see Gadi's directing skills firsthand while he was filming a feature in Israel, *Green Fields*, a film about the futility of the intifada, and his obvious talent as a director was made crystal clear to me. In 1993, Channel Four in the U.K. ran a "Maps and Dreams" series showing different films from both Arab and Israeli filmmakers each week, and one week there was a documentary called "The Men Who Say No to the Cinema," and it was about Israeli filmmakers and the ironic fact that they receive money from what was then a right-wing Likud government to produce films which are left-wing in content. Even more ironic was the fact that Ariel Sharon, who had allowed the Sabra and Shatilla massacre to unfold in Lebanon, was, at that particular time, the minister of Commerce and Industry and therefore the power behind the funding. "The Men Who Say No to the Cinema" contained a large segment about the film *Green Fields*, and there was Gadi filming it, and the entire documentary was dedicated to him. (The film *Delta Force II* was also dedicated to him and the four others who died while filming it.) As Dahn Ben Amotz lay on his deathbed, an Israeli film distributor who had known him and who had been inspired by the article about me in the paper, bought the rights himself for a 'song.'

This was soon after the helicopter crash, so I had lost Gadi, lost my project and had shared him, not only it seemed, with his wife but with yet another woman. Rachel was graduating from high school and had a nine-month respite until she was due to serve her two-year stint in the Israel Defence Forces. My parents told me that they were very proud of all I had accomplished in Israel, would be pleased if we returned to the States, and would help us in any way they could to reestablish ourselves there.

Right around that time I met a very evolved soul named Rami. We spoke of many things, and I expressed my anger at losing the *To Remember, to Forget* project, and he said something to me that, at the time, I didn't fully understand, "That book is in the old. You are meant to be working in the new. In a few years, films, books, television and, yes, even newspapers and magazines will be totally changed. People will be searching for true spirituality and you will be a beacon of light for them and you will have a part in helping to bring the 'exiles' home once again."

This conversation took place late summer 1989. Who could have known what was about to unfold? Books like Shirley MacLaine's *Out on a Limb*, Betty J. Eadie's *Embraced by the Light* and James Redfield's *Celestine*

Prophecy would not be published for a few years. Films like *Ghost*, *Michael*, and *Phenomenon* brought spirituality to the mainstream, along with TV's *X-Files*, *Millennium* and *Touched by an Angel*. Who could have predicted that in 1997 the endearing *Touched by an Angel* would be rated as the scond most popular TV show after-*ER*? Or that Art Bell's cutting edge late-night radio show — *Coast to Coast* — would attract 15 million listeners ready and willing to take part in experiential odysseys and metaphysical calesthenics five hours a night, six days a week?

So when Rami told me I would have a part in helping to bring "exiles" home I felt like a homeless exile myself; even though I understood that a teacher had appeared, this pupil was not yet ready. What I really wanted was to meet Rinat and, since we had already spoken on the phone a few times, she finally agreed to meet me one evening right before I left Israel.

And the king loved Esther more than all the other women, and she obtained grace and favor in his sight more than all the other virgins, so that he set the royal crown upon her head and made her queen instead of Vashti.

Esther 2:17

IX

The Other Woman

Rinat and I met at a coffee shop in Tel Aviv; we sat for about five hours and talked. One of the things we both realized was that Gadi had told us both "half truths."

I rarely asked Gadi any of the usual "who, what, where, when" questions. Even then I knew enough about astrology to understand that Gadi, an Aquarius, was too detached to give his Leo wife the devotion she demanded. Leo's egos need time and attention and stroking, but unfortunately the jealousy of Leo women can be all-encompassing. Gadi was an air sign, like me, and so I understood too well that ours was a spontaneous relationship with the pressure off; we both needed to breathe freely. So I can't say that he ever lied to me, he just omitted telling me that he had left his wife and was living with Rinat.

Rinat was also a Leo, like Gadi's wife, although she was twenty years or so her junior. The Leo/Aquarius relationship often is a love-at-first-sight one for these two magnetic zodiac opposites. As Rinat began to speak about her relationship with Gadi, I was struck by the fact that Gadi, who was surprisingly concerned about aging, had probably relived with Rinat the early days of his courtship with his wife. One newspaper article after his death spoke about "the most handsome soldier married the prettiest female soldier...and they were married at 21."

Retin-A, that acne cream which miraculously eliminates lines and wrinkles, was available over-the-counter under the name Airol, and when Gadi saw a tube on my night table he asked me to get him some. He was forty-four at the time and looked at least ten years younger. I used to tease him when I hadn't seen him for a while by counting the new gray hairs on his chest. About a month after the crash, I had lunch with a director who'd worked with Gadi for years. "You know," he said to me over hummus and techina, "Gadi was someone I could never imagine growing old...just the thought of him bald, or with a beer belly or prostate problems was an impossible thought."

I know that Rinat expected not to like me, but as we spoke I could sense that she was warming up to me. After all, we had both loved the same man, and for a few hours we were able to glimpse at each other's mirror. Suddenly she looked at me and said softly, "When I was angry with him, I wouldn't let him come near me. You never did that; you were always there for him. I withheld sex; you didn't." When she asked me how I met Gadi, I was transported back in time to ten years earlier.

I ran a Jerusalem-based advertising/public relations agency and one of our clients was a resort hotel in the holiday town of Netanya. The late Moshe Dayan's son, Assie, was making a film called *King for a Day*. In Israel these are called "boureka films," named for a type of pastry which, even though there's a cheese or potato filling, expands in the oven so that it seems to be filled with air. Dayan asked me if he could film in the hotel for four weeks during the slow winter season. The hotel's general manager agreed, and I suggested that we take advantage of the filming process and have them cover the cost of filming and editing a separate promotional film for the hotel, which was needed to sell the hotel abroad. Everyone was in agreement, and I offered to write the script and act as producer.

It was an adorable concept: two kids about seven years old come to the hotel for a holiday and the viewer sees all the hotel facilities through their eyes. I set the whole thing up for a weekend shoot, commandeered Rachel and a friend's son to be the actors, and we drove up to Netanya one Friday afternoon. There I was told that a director/cameraman would meet us at the Blue Bay Hotel. And that was how I met Gadi.

I was drawn to him immediately, with a feeling that I had known him before, but dismissed it as wishful thinking. I was living with Manny, who was perhaps the only person I have ever been able to describe as "the salt of the earth," and he loved me so much. Manny and I met right after my arrival in Israel in 1978. I was employed as spokesperson for the United Jewish Appeal and Manny was the assistant to the director of the UJA. I had been divorced for three years and the five-year marriage, in which the term "mental cruelty" became alive for me in all its facets, had left me feeling betrayed and hurt. Manny's love for me healed the emotional scars left over from that marriage.

As I was relating to Rinat how I met Gadi, I told her that three things from that weekend in Netanya stayed with me. The first scene of the promotional film showed the kids arriving by bus to the hotel where they would then check in. Rachel was carrying one of these small square suitcases — the kind that once was used for make-up. When she came to the reception desk she must have realized that she was about a head shorter than her male "co-star" and didn't reach the top of the reception desk and was therefore unable to sign in. She immediately put the case she was carrying on the floor and climbed on top of it, thereby giving herself about 10 inches of additional height, and Gadi's camera went immediately to her impromptu movements, with a close-up of her feet climbing on the suitcase.

By the third and final day of shooting, both kids were tired and coming down with colds, but Gadi managed to keep them amused and in top form as we filmed the last scene at the Blue Bay Hotel's stables. Both kids were given a pan of fodder and were directed to feed the horses. From the left stall, one horse was happily eating away when suddenly two things happened at the ame moment. Gadi's two small daughters — who were about four and six years old — appeared along with their mother. They ran up to their daddy, who was in the middle of filming, and each girl grabbed a denim-clad leg to hug, clamoring for his attention. At the same time, the previously unseen horse from the right-hand stall appeared and — surprise, surprise–two horses were eating out of Rachel's pan and she broke into a huge smile that made her adorable dimple quite prominent. Gadi, without disturbing his daughters, got the shot. Not only did he allow his daughters to cling to him, but through his smile and his body language I saw that he did so without anger and with infinite compassion. At that time I never thought to ask myself why Gadi's wife allowed the children to disturb him in the middle of work… I just saw how lovingly he handled what would easily have been the loss of the best shot of the film…and at that precise moment I fell in love with him.

כל העולם
כולו גשר
צר מאד
והעיקר לא
לפחד כלל

There is no man who has power over the wind to withhold the wind; neither has he power over the day of death; and there is no escape from duty in the day of battle; neither shall wickedness deliver those who are given to it. All this have I seen, and applied my heart to every work that is done under the sun; there is a time when one man rules under another to hurt him.

Ecclesiastes 8:8-9

X

The Path Widens

ב In February 1989, Gadi returned from Kenya, where he'd spent a month filming a nature documentary, I was temporarily living in a hotel in Tel Aviv with Rachel while we waited for our apartment to become available. Before he left for Kenya, I asked him what was going on with our relationship, and he said, "I'm not in a space right now where I can deal with this." I accepted the fact that he was working things out and respected his honesty.

A few months earlier, my friend Mira, one of Israel's leading astrologers, offered to give Gadi an astrological reading. I'd first met Mira in 1986, during a period that Gadi and I had stopped seeing each other for about eleven months. His wife found out about us and he couldn't handle the situation. We had been involved for two years at that point. I remember telling Mira that Gadi wanted to resume the relationship and that, although the attraction was stronger than ever, the truth was that I had managed for nearly a year without him, and I didn't see the point of getting involved again if there was no future. Mira did what she called a "soul comparison chart" and said that Gadi and I were soul mates from many incarnations and that, somehow, we would always be together. Before she would give him a reading, however, she wanted to know when his wife's birthday was so that she could prepare and compare our three charts. Strange as it sounds, Gadi didn't know when his wife's birthday was. "Sometime in August," he told me. Gadi had been married to the same woman for 23 years and he really didn't know the date of her birth.

When we would have the session with Miriam a few months later, he would say, "Listen, once a year I get into bed with the fear of death…it passes within half an hour…once a year…once in two years…I assume that this happens to everyone. But when I get into a car or do my army reserve duty, then I'm afraid that something will happen to me — that I'll die — I ask the drivers to drive slowly."

"Since when?" asked Miriam. "A year ago, yesterday?"

"A few years ago — since the public awareness shows that so many people here die from traffic accidents, I get into the car and ask the driver to drive slowly, carefully. I go to the army, I'm one of the soldiers that doesn't sleep all night…I say, 'just me the fucking terrorists will get'… Up until today, touch wood, nothing has happened…once I was in a near-fatal accident but it ended okay, and it was an accident that could have ended in death for me and my wife — she saved us."

"When?" asked Miriam.

He said, "I can tell you the area."

"No," she replied. "I mean the year, month – when?"

"Years ago in '73 or '74. It was nearly winter. Listen, you're speaking to someone who doesn't know his kids' birthdays, his wife's, his parents' — no one's."

When I drove him to Jerusalem for his astrological reading with Mira, we passed a horrific accident on the highway (which we later found out had taken the life of one of the youngest members of the Israeli Parliament). I was actually looking forward to sitting in on this session. I hoped that it would shed some light on my relationship with him — it was nearly impossible to talk with him about anything of "consequence." Whenever I broached the subject of his marriage or our relationship, he would either put his finger on my lips, or his lips on my lips…either way seemed destined to start something that was not a serious discussion. Once we got to Jerusalem and to Mira, Gadi decided that I was not to be privy to this reading, so I spent two hours window shopping and being generally pissed off. On the way back to Tel Aviv, he shared precious little with me about the reading. About a half hour out of Jerusalem, he asked me to turn into the Jerusalem Forest, and we got out of the car. I thought that he wanted to go for a walk, but no, he wanted to "have his way with me" right there, minutes away from where we had seen the fatal car crash just a few hours earlier.

That entire area — the Jerusalem Corridor — was permeated with death and pain. In the film *Cast a Giant Shadow*, Kirk Douglas plays Colonel Mickey Marcus in the true story of the ill-fated American soldier who volunteers to come to Israel in 1948 during the War of Independence. Jerusalem's population had been cut off from the rest of the country by Arabs, and he is to help the newly formed Israeli Army build a road through the Jerusalem Corridor to allow desperately needed water and food supplies through to a starving population. The highway to Jerusalem, as one starts the hilly climb, is still strewn with tanks and memorial placards in remembrance of the soldiers who didn't make it.

The more I was to study and investigate spirituality, the more I would understand that much of Israel's angst and pain comes from the confusion surrounding the "law of return." Any Israeli will tell you that the law of return states that any Jew from anywhere in the world is automatically granted Israeli citizenship (assuming that his or her mother was Jewish) once they arrive in Israel. In fact, I believe that the law of karma is the law of return. Anything we put out will return to us. The reason we've created karma, or results of actions in past lives, is to increase our understanding, and understanding ultimately can transcend our karmic circumstances which, in any event, arose out of our ignorance.

Not very far from the spot where Gadi was ravishing me beneath the Jerusalem pines is a place called Latrun, which is known for its lovely monastery nestled among lush green trees and colorful flowers. There the monks have taken a vow of silence and, as far as I know, the only one who is allowed to talk is the one who sells the wine and liquor which, as far as many Israelis are concerned, is what the monastery is there for. But Latrun is also known as one of the bloodiest battlegrounds during the War of Independence in 1948, where hundreds of Israelis died. What is not as generally well-known is that during that time the newborn State of Israel was desperate for arms and just as desperate for soldiers. So, while the war was raging and right after the British partitioned Palestine into an Arab and Jewish State, the Arabs outnumbered the Jews ten to one. Boats started arriving from Cyprus that were filled with holocaust survivors, the remnants of European Jewry, six million of their brethren destroyed, and these wretched souls had been denied access to Palestine by the British since 1945. So not only had they lived through the horrors of the concentration camps in Europe, they then had to suffer the added indignity of an internment camp in Cyprus for three years until they were finally brought to the fledgling state. And as soon as they arrived they were given army uniforms and weapons and sent immediately to fight the battle of Latrun. According to the "law of return" they were Israelis the moment they arrived at their homeland and they, of course, were the hundreds of "Israelis" who died at Latrun.

Just as we all have our individual karmas, so, too, is there national karma. We commonly think of karma as a system of rewards, and when life gets tough we ask, "Why me? I must have 'bad karma!'" And what this does is keep us very close to our egos. According to Kevin Ryerson and Stephanie Harolde's book, *Spirit Communication—the Soul's Path* (Kevin Ryerson featured prominently in Shirley MacLaine's *Out on a Limb*, and of his book she says, "This is the clearest and most comprehensive book on the phenomenon of channeling I've ever read!"):

"Bad karma gives us very little freedom because it sets obstacles in our path. Good karma affords lots of freedom because the road always seems wide open. But whether we're dealing with bad karma, and very little freedom, or good karma, and lots of freedom, we're still dealing with degrees of freedom. Enlightenment, or ultimate realization, is total liberation, total freedom. Bad karma and good karma both tie us to conditional mind because they cause us to judge ourselves. People with good karma can fall prey to thinking they're better than others ('I have good karma, so therefore I must be special'). People with bad karma tend to have low self-esteem and see themselves as worse than others ('My bad karma is punishment for being such a bad person'). This is the wrong perception. It's a form of divine behaviorism — condition and response. It's functioning from the basis of the ego.

"To rise above this ball and chain, we have to eliminate the ego.

The only way to eliminate the ego is to go outside of it. And what lies outside the ego is God. Karma has only one value — to increase our understanding of our true nature as children of God. Once we understand who we are, we don't need to create karma, either positive or negative. Once we understand who we are, karma is eliminated, because its only purpose is to increase our understanding. The reason for every experience in our lives is to increase our understanding. The fulfillment of karma is synonymous with enlightenment, and enlightenment is remembering who we are, remembering our own true nature."

According to Buddhist psychology, the same concepts apply; that is in order to transform ourselves in the here and now, we must eliminate the ego. The Buddhist Four Noble Truths state:

All life contains suffering.
All suffering is based on desire.
All desire arises out of ego.
The way to eliminate desire is to eliminate the ego.

There is a well-known transchannel whom I knew in Israel. A few books deal with her work, which consists of channeling from a group of universal beings. They state that what has gone wrong on Planet Earth is that, instead of learning to balance between the physical and the spiritual worlds, which is why the Earth was created, Planet Earth has become a place of desire. Love generates the energy that feeds God, and this planet has stopped the growth of part of the Universe because souls have become involved in materialism. Their desires are still in their minds and emotions, and their desire holds them to this planet.

The transchannel also told me something that resonated quite deeply with me: that the one million children who perished in the holocaust reincarnated as Israelis! The reason I could relate to this information was that although the aggression and pushiness of the Israelis is second to none, what underlies this nation's "chutzpah" is an almost childlike naiveté coupled with the need to judge everyone and everything, and in judging others we reflect our own lack of self-worth. And there is lots of fear there, lots of "faith in the negative." I've often thought that if Israelis could relate to this information, they might then be ready to forgive, and every person we forgive adds to our own self-love. When we put out positive thoughts, they return to us, so it's worthwhile to do what we perceive as positive to one another — not out of motivation to ward off bad karma, but with the understanding that we've created everything in our lives to increase our understanding of who we are. This is the very point at which we begin to fulfill our purpose. To quote Kevin Ryerson: "When we understand that karma exists strictly to increase our understanding, the karma itself is fulfilled. Out of our understanding, we realize that we're unlimited beings, that we are a part of that being called God. And this is the human condition."

I believe that on a soul level I understood this even though I was just beginning my spiritual search and was still caught up in various and sundry "dramas." I said to the woman who gave me this information, "I do believe that many Israelis could relate to this concept that they are the reincarnations of the one million children who died in the holocaust... how healing it would be for everyone to understand the holocaust in those terms. It could help bring about a major shift in consciousness, and it would bring peace to an area which has been caught up in suffering, death and pain since 1948." To which she became quite annoyed with me and said, "This is information I have received — you're not allowed to use this in your book!" To paraphrase Marshall McLuhan: The medium is not always the message!

And the light of Israel shall be for a fire, and his Holy One for a flame; and it shall burn and devour his thorns and his briers in one day...

For though your people Israel be as the sand of the sea, yet a remnant of them shall return; their number decreased, cut off, but flooded with righteousness.

Isaiah 11:17,22

XI

Unconditional Love

In the spring of 1993, I left the UK and returned to Santa Fe, where I'd lived for a year after leaving Israel in 1989, to visit my daughter. I had just spent two years in England where I was able to come terms with my relationship with Gadi and start to put in perspective all that had happened to me since he had "passed over." Perhaps one of the most important things I've come to understand through my spiritual search — and ultimately have come to believe — is that we choose our lives before we incarnate, for the lessons we need to learn.

My daugher Rachel, when she was quite young, showed an interest in the holocaust that belied her years. Although her Savta (grandmother) and Sabba (grandfather) in Israel had indeed lived through it, they spoke very little of their experiences during the war. When she was about twelve, I took her to meet a Canadian-Israeli producer I had met at the Cannes film festival who was visiting her parents in Israel. As we were leaving, Rachel spotted a framed photograph of a family and asked my friend's father who they were. He was a man well into his sixties and he told her that this was his family, all of whom had perished in the holocaust; he was the sole survivor. I was already downstairs when Rachel came down, shaken and crying. "What's the matter?" I asked her, and she told me that when my friend's father told her that he had lost all his family in the holocaust, she was so moved that she went to give him a hug and, as she did, he tried to "French kiss" her. She was terribly upset, as well as angry, and I could only console her with empty platitudes.

A few years later, John Demanjuk was brought to Israel to stand trial, and the trial was televised every day. I followed it religiously, and what stands out in my mind, more than anything else, were the survivors and the pain, hurt and, especially, the anger, all synonyms for fear. Even when the Israeli Supreme Court, in a landmark decision, acquitted Demanjuk of the charge that he was Ivan the Terrible, the anger and the pain of those survivors (who had in fact identified the wrong man under oath) had not abated; in fact, they seemed angrier than ever. There are no words that any one of us who has not lived through the horrors of that time could offer as consolation to these angry and broken old men. But for me, I have come to understand the power and the healing that emerges from our ability to forgive. Forgiveness is the ultimate liberator, freeing us from the burdens of hatred, but like grief, it is a process.

Christopher Bache, in his excellent book *Lifecycles*, writes:

"Forgiveness is an extremely powerful means of clearing karma from our lives. To genuinely forgive is to assert great power and control over our destiny. Perhaps for this reason it is such a universal theme in the world's religions: 'Forgive our sins as we forgive those who sin against us.' 'Judge not and you shall not be judged." On all continents, the refrain appears: as you forgive, so shall you be forgiven. Often what we are asked to forgive in others are the same failings we have come to recognize in ourselves, for here too we find the field effect operating.

The ethical teachings of the world's religions are remarkably consistent. The fundamental values of compassion, fair play, and forgiveness seem universally distributed. We are told that we should meet whatever happens to us with equanimity and forbearance. In all our dealings with each other, we should follow the Golden Rule. By adopting this principle of equal-regard, we break the cycles of karma that are rippling through our lives from a past we can no longer see. By treating others as we wish to be treated, by not responding to evil with evil, we right the wrongs of the past and deepen our awareness of the underlying unity of life. Above all, we should know that we are safe, that nothing could possibly separate us permanently from the source of our life, and that the rigors of life are ultimately for our own benefit."

When the Holocaust Museum opened in Washington, DC, I read in the *New York Times* of a young, gay, German man who stayed on in Washington after the Gay Rights Convention in order to visit the museum. Everyone who enters the museum is given the name of a person of their sex who perished in the holocaust, and then they follow the last years or months of that person's life as they go through the museum. It seems that this young man was given the name of a young gay man, a non-Jew like himself, who was murdered by the Nazis because he was homosexual. In the interview, the man said that the experience was the most profound thing he had ever experienced, and then he said that his grandfather, who had been a Nazi sympathizer, to this day still hates Jews.

In Santa Fe, Rachel asked me if I would meet her teacher, the man who taught the Holocaust course she had just completed. She said that he had expressed an interest in the book I was writing and wanted to meet me.

When we met for lunch, he was totally effusive over Rachel and was kind enough to share with me the feelings he experienced by having the grandchild of survivors as a participant in his course. He viewed her, unlike himself or any other of the participants in the course, as a child of the very events that were studied and as someone who, given her lineal and literal history, need not only peer through the gates that Elie Wiesel speaks of but who, at least in the metaphysical sense, can even pass through them, stand amid the carnage of the holocaust, and be directly touched by its impact. Rachel had shared with him times she had spent with her Savta and Sabba as a small child and what those recollected moments mean to her now as a young woman, amid the shadow of events which were studied in the course. He felt that she had, on a certain level, suffered from the impact of her grandparents' experiences; that since most of those experiences had been only alluded to, communicating to her only unspoken fear and pain, she became so unnerved by her inner voices that she did not know what to do with her reactions.

He told me that she had written in one of her papers: "I'm edgy and nervous, because I know that each time I walk into class as a student,

I walk out of there as a Jew, and that follows me into my life now." He wrote in his comments on her final exam paper: "Of course you are more than just a Jew — unlike any of the rest of us, you are something of a true survivor, born of and descended from the fires of those awful events. Like your shadow, that fact, that fate, will always be a part of you, always there, impossible either to evade or to touch. That can't but haunt, and I suspect that you are a long way from coming to terms with it... I know that there is an entire side of you that I have never seen, even though I've spent a fair amount of time poking around, looking for it. 'It' is a part of you that, I suspect, you don't show much, even to yourself. 'It' is filled with questions, questions, questions–and there is not much there in the way of answers. Sharp edges, inexplicable bitterness, perplexity — no safe spots or secure handholds. All those unanswered questions must generate a fair amount of unrelenting and unrelieved anxiety."

Somehow I had the distinct feeling that he was mirroring much of his own "unrelenting and unrelieved anxiety" through the only student in his class who could ask him to confront his own ghosts. He ended his memorandum by telling her: "Some day, some time, some place, you will need to confront your ghosts, to look for the answers–for only the truth will set you free, and I don't think you've found it yet...I'm pleased to give you an 'A' for a course grade–you've earned it several times over." Maybe his ghosts still needed confronting, but he certainly could recognize a smart kid!

I began to think about the fact that Rachel had been so influenced by the relatively few times she had spent with her Israeli grandparents and, once again, was struck by the almost simplistic, yet powerful, idea that small children can't think, that they only feel, and how this fact alone is the number one factor that causes so very many people to grow up carrying the emotional baggage from birth or from age two, three or four with them, without understanding how enormously heavy that baggage becomes after twenty, thirty, forty, or more years of "schlepping" it around, and how this baggage, once recognized, confronted and released, is the only way we can truly begin to love ourselves totally and unconditionally. In Rachel's case, there was perhaps the fear she had picked up from her grandparents, but somehow I didn't feel that this alone was enough to account for her unusual preoccupation with the holocaust.

When I first moved to Santa Fe, I met Susan Harris, author of *Theater of the Soul*, a Jewish psychologist who had recently completed some work in which she was able to view her past lives through the psychospiritual work she was doing. "I saw myself being herded into a gas chamber, along with hundreds of others," she told me, "and then, the very next moment, I saw myself sitting here, in Santa Fe, and I thought: 'Ha, so this is what it's all about... I died in a moment and here I am, alive, totally enjoying my life, so what's the big deal, and what a lot of fear people feed into regarding death,' and at that moment I understood that we are truly immortal beings, that the body may die, but the soul is back in another body in what seemed to me to be the blink of an eye."

The feeling that Rachel had a past life during the holocaust seemed more and more likely to me. The comments her teacher made seemed almost as if, on a soul level, he, too, sensed it.

Then, of course, there was the metaphysical idea that the million children who died at that time reincarnated as Israelis. Rachel was an Israeli and often exhibited seemingly groundless fears which never had a logical explanation. Her hypochondria was source of amusement to me. Once, when she was about fifteen, she stepped on a thumbtack that had fallen out of its package — perhaps one-sixteenth of an inch had actually penetrated her foot. She was convinced that she had lockjaw — for two days she told me that her jaw hurt and that she couldn't open her mouth properly. According to Louise Hay's *Heal Your Body*, lockjaw (real or, as in this case, imagined) is caused by "a need to release angry, festering thoughts." And, particularly during her teenage years in Israel, her fears and anger often seemed to manifest with an intensity I could not fathom.

Her early years, while far from perfect, nonetheless seemed to have had none of the traumas which we have come to associate with emotional scarring. When I was pregnant, in 1971, Fitzhugh Dodson's groundbreaking book *How to Parent* had just been published, which was very lucky for all of us baby boomers whose parents still believed that babies needed to cry "because their lungs need exercise"! And, although I worked, I was teaching only twelve hours a week until she was five, and my divorce when she was three was handled with a minimum of angst. And, until we went to live in Israel when she was six-and-a-half, we lived close to my parents, and, as the first grandchild, she benefited from an extremely close and loving relationship with her grandparents. However, from the time she turned fifteen until her nineteenth year there were, indeed, times I felt as if I was living through a mini-holocaust of my own with her and, indeed, it was only my new understanding, around that time, of the concept of unconditional love which enabled me to maintain my sanity.

It happened one Saturday morning. I had dreamed of a magnificent rainbow and somehow sensed a shift in my perception, since it is rare that I remember dreams. That morning, while Rachel was going on about something in a tone that was both abusive and obtrusive, I noticed that I was suddenly listening to her, not reacting in kind, and not thinking what a mess her room was or how she was going to flunk out of school or that she was staying out too late. I just stood there and thought: "I love this child exactly the way she is," and as I had this thought Rachel said, "What's with you?" and I said, "I love you unconditionally," and she said, "More of your new age shit — it won't last." But it did. And it has.

Of course, it took Rachel about six more years to come to understand that although I may not have been the kind of mother her grandmother thought I should be, I was exactly the mother she had chosen because of the lessons she needed. When I went to England when she was nineteen, to write this book, my mother had informed Aunty Vera and the other English cousins that I had, in effect, deserted my daughter in order to pursue my crazy dreams. When I was invited to dinner with the new in-laws of my favourite cousin, Jon, in London, they asked how old my child was. "Nineteen," I replied, and noted that they seemed surprised. Later, Jon told me that his in-laws were indeed surprised because they had heard, via the "Jewish grapevine," that I had run off to England, deserting my "small" child (who had already completed her first year of college and was thinking about taking an apartment with her boyfriend). Actually, the two-year separation (but for a summer break together) was probably the best thing I could have done for both of us. I was still healing from the death of Gadi, his apparent duplicity, and other residuals from those last few years of living in the "Holy Land."

After the lunch with Professor Warren, I decided to have a session with the Santa Fe-based transchannel Rand Lee, who had said to me two years earlier, "I've never yet met a Jewish person who has not had a past life during the holocaust."

Then the dust shall return to the earth as it was;
and the spirit shall return to God who gave it.

For the Lord shall bring every work into judgment,
concerning everything which is hidden and known,
whether it be good or whether it be evil.

Ecclesiastes 12:7,14

XII

Past Lives & the Holocaust

June 2, 1993
Santa Fe, New Mexico

Mommy dearest,

May you have an incredible birthday and a magnificent year. May luck and success come your way and smile upon your soul. You have really helped me very much at actualizing myself and given me much faith and hope. You are an incredible person who is indeed a little crazy, but your pursuit of happiness and of your dreams is really commendable. I love you very much, my free-spirited mom...it may have taken me years to realize your uniqueness, but what's 21 years when you're as old as you are. Ha!

Much love,
Rachel

When Rachel gave me this birthday message, she couldn't understand why I began to cry, and I said that I never could have imagined, after everything she had put me through during her teenage years—and in particular, as I embarked on my spiritual path (and she was so closed to anything I wanted to share with her)—that one day she would actually thank me! When I told her this she looked at me in surprise. She honestly didn't remember being so hurtful and negative. Although she was wishing for a mother who spent her days in the kitchen making chicken soup and matzo balls, in truth it was only when we returned to the States after twelve years in Israel that her perception of me altered.

For me, coming back to the States was in many ways akin to arriving in a foreign land. There was a vocabulary I didn't recognize, words I couldn't find in my 1979 edition of the pocket *Webster*. Words like *dysfunctional*, and *12-step*, and *co-dependent* (when I came to understand the meaning of co-dependent, however, I realized that Israel is possibly the most co-dependent country in the world with a population of 4 million, which includes 2 million Jewish mothers!). For Rachel, too, it was a new land where nearly everyone she was meeting had been either sexually abused or emotionally starved, or had been a druggie or an alcoholic or battered as a child. America had changed, and I was looking better and better in Rachel's eyes. I guess she figured it's preferable to have a mother who goes into an altered state when she talks about numerology than a mother like her friend Shawn's, who kicked him out of the house because he wouldn't agree to deal drugs for her boyfriend.

A few days after my birthday (notice I'm not saying which birthday; I believe that a woman's age, weight and checking account balance are protected by the First Amendment), I went to see Rand Lee. After a very positive reading of the Tarot cards, he went into trance: after a minute or two his voice altered and he said, "We thank you for sharing. Your first question involves Rachel and her connection with the holocaust, and it is true that there is a past-life experience in this period for her. Do you have a specific question concerning this?"

Although I'd had a couple of readings with Rand two and a half years earlier, he hardly remembered me when I came this time, and he had never met my daughter. I asked, "Who was she specifically during this period? Was she a child, a man or a woman? May I please have some details?" And did I ever get details!

"What we see is a connection to Poland [Rachel's father is Polish], and a Polish background. We see a camp where a great many Polish individuals were sent for death and we do not necessarily see Jewish, but one of the others who was sent. We are seeing several individuals — one individual seems to be a German or Austrian soldier in uniform who is particularly brutal and hostile, perhaps one of the guards at the camp, or a sentry; next we see a young girl of perhaps eighteen or nineteen years old with dark hair and dark eyes; next we see an old woman who is very thin and emaciated with her hair bound up with lice and scabs on the body and she appears to be scrubbing a floor. We will ask what these images mean."

While Rand was silently accessing the details from the group intelligence he works with, I thought of a few occasions when Rachel was younger and how when she was angry she seemed to be particularly brutal and hostile. I thought about her extreme attraction to fleas (i.e., if there was even one flea in someone's house, it went straight to Rachel's ankle). And, although I know it's part of being a "normal" teenager to have a messy room, the state of Rachel's room defied comparison to any kid's room I'd ever seen — it was almost as if to clean it was metaphysically painful to her.

Rand continued his channeling: "The woman who is now Rachel had, indeed, a significant connection to this period, but it may be difficult for us to explain how an individual can have three past lives in the same time period, so it is necessary for you to realize that incarnation is not linear — at death you can reenter space/time at any point in history. In other words, let us say that if you die in the year 2030 and you go back to the center of the dream state and relive your life and make different plans for your next life, you can come back into physical reality at any point in history — in 10,000 BC or 20,000 AD or even in the year you were born as Sunny in this incarnation. Conceivably, you can even grow up as a next-door neighbor of Sunny in this incarnation and know yourself (although this is extremely rare). For you, Sunny would be a past life even though you were living in the same time period...like a time traveler who goes back and has the experience of getting to know her grandmother, although from the grandmother's point of view they are contemporaries. Does this make sense intellectually? Because space/time is elastic, there is room for all desired experiences — if not in this time/space continuum, then in a parallel universe."

This theory was not brand new to me; in my previous reading with Rand, he had told me that I, too, had two parallel lives, one as a Roman gentleman around the year 70 AD who was sent to the Middle East as part of a contingency from Rome. He was a man who had a childhood of confusing dreams...where a lion would speak to him and tell him he was going far away and that he would do a thing that would shake the world, and later dreams of seven lamps that floated above the head of the lion and seven oil jars at the feet of the lion, and of the earthquake that shatters them all. At the hill fortress of Masada, where he was sent with others of the Roman force, he realized that his dream was about to take place, for as he looked up at the hill it became a lion with seven stars at its brow, seven lamps above its head, and seven oil jars at its foot. Although he is afraid, he climbs up the fortress with the others where they find that all are dead, and he feels great shame and anguish, because of the women's and children's deaths. And suddenly he comes upon seven oil jars and seven lamps, and within each jar are scrolls. The captain orders that the scrolls be taken away, but the Roman gentleman takes one and hides it in his cloak and brings it back with him to Rome, and this is the only scroll that was not destroyed.

According to Rand, "You were used by God himself to save one of them — the one scroll that describes the most secret revelations of the time of peace and upheaval — and we believe that you became a Roman in this incarnation so that you would live to find the scroll where your fellows could not."

Then Rand told me that, in the same period, I was also a young woman at Masada and, just as Rachel's reading had great relevance to her present life, so this information was for me a gateway to understanding some of the whys and wherefores of my present life.

My father, who for much of his life had worked as a shochet or ritual slaughterer, said, when we returned from Israel (the week the Berlin wall came down) that there was some information originating, he thought, from the Dead Sea Scrolls which, when it becomes known, will turn world religions totally upside down. His words had haunted me, and I had begun a serious inquiry into the scrolls and, more important, into the Essenes, the group reputed to have written them.

So I was unnerved when Rand continued, "You were the daughter and there were five children in the family. Your father was one of a council, not the most secret Essene council, but a council of some authority in arranging the community, and understand that it was with his hand that he killed you. And you knew what must be borne. The only moment of weakness that you had, according to you, was when you saw him raise his hand to the infant and a word escaped your lips. One word only, and you saw it shake him as if a knife had gone through his heart. And so you shut your mouth and longed for the knife itself. You have been carrying the guilt of that word for life after life and that is why you have chosen a life in which no one will listen to your words, for before God and the people you blamed yourself for causing your father, who was in the greatest of all distresses possible, to lose for a moment his resolve, and thus you felt that God himself would punish you. You have often felt that your words would bring down a great disaster, and this we see as the root. It is not such a great thing, but to a child, in conditions of unimaginable stress and peril, it is the greatest of scars on the soul, and your first role to be successful is to forgive yourself for this utterance."

When I asked what the utterance was I was told that it is in a language not lodged in Mr. Lee's range, but that it is one syllable in the Hebrew alphabet beginning a word, and that it is a symbol of mystic significance. It took me a few days before I was able to handle this...I had memories of my father, after he sharpened the knife that he used to cut the jugular of the steers, according to the biblical laws of Jewish ritual slaughtering, pulling a hair from my head and holding the hair in his hand, up in the air, and brandishing his knife in mid air. If the hair was cut in two, then his knife was sharp enough.

By the time I had that reading with Rand, I had learned that I was not responsible for my infant brother's death, but I did not yet know that I told my mother Michael was crying and she did not listen to me. When I went through the Hebrew alphabet a few days later, trying to figure out which letter would have formed a word which would have caused my father such pain (and me two thousand years of guilt), I stopped suddenly with the eighth letter of the Hebrew alphabet—the letter "chet"..." ח ", The word "chet" means sin.

So my openness to Rachel's past-life reading with Rand Lee was not surprising. He continued, "The woman, Rachel, has had three incarnations in the holocaust period, and it appears that she had attempted three different lives in order to understand the period; one of an old woman in the camp who we feel was perhaps mentally retarded, who was sent to work scrubbing floors, and, in a way that might seem impossible to you today, survived the holocaust and has felt very guilty and angry that she survived while so many young and beautiful wasted away before her eyes. Second, a girl in the full blossoming of youth who was molested in the camp and ended her life in a violent manner; and, third, as a guard, a male, who was a sentry in the camp, pacing on the outside wall, above the camp, whose job it was to oversee individuals attempting to escape, to keep an eye out for danger; and so we feel that there are at least three lives connected to this period, possibly in the same camp. In important periods of history, space and time do strange things and in the concentration camps, for example, the precise metaphysics of space/time have never been properly understood in our reality."

I asked if the young girl or the old woman had been Jewish.

Rachel had been in a relationship with Adam, a non-Jew, for a few years. The very last letter I received from my dad, a few weeks before he "physically passed over" was an admonition...how could I allow Rachel, who has such a love of Judaism, to be involved with a "goy"? My love for Adam transcended any religious dogmas, and so I decided to ignore the letter. (When Rachel and I returned from Israel, I remember having a discussion one day with some friends, and someone used the word "dogma." Rachel asked what it meant [her English vocabulary was somewhat lacking; after all, she'd gone from the second grade through her high school matriculation in another language]. "Dogma," we explained to her, "is a formal tenet or principle, an authoritative doctrine of a church." She thought for a moment and then said, "When you spell dogma backwards, it's 'am God'...is that the opposite of 'dogma'?")

Rand answered my question: "The old woman appears to have been Polish and was a Gentile of Catholic background...the young dark-haired woman appears to have had a Jewish connection — her dark coloring suggests possibly a Romany connection — and the man who was the sentry was a Polish family man of a phlegmatic temperament, not particularly intelligent, and angry because of the economic depression in his country — what you in America would call a kind of redneck."

I asked Rand, "And Rachel's boyfriend, Adam—is he connected in any way to the holocaust?"

"He was her boyfriend when she was the dark-haired Jewish girl. He appears to have been a non-Jew of sandy-blond hair, separated from her when they took her away. Because she was part Romany, there was some prejudice against her...she grew up with a fiery and rebellious temperament (for a moment I thought he was talking about Rachel in her present life!). She was killed in the camp in an escape attempt, shot by the guard who was a future incarnation of herself, and the old lady was one of those pressed into service to push the bodies into a common grave. And so the woman, Rachel, has incarnated both as the girl who was shot on the attempt, the rifleman who shot her, and the old woman who buried her body."

"And what is that meant to tell us?"

"In Rachel's case, since she has lived many incarnations with great fear of death, it was a way of learning that death is not as simple as it seems to be to the judgemental mind; that in a way, we are our own mother and father — we bring ourselves into the world and take ourselves out of it, and there is within each human being the capacity for every act, whether evil or good. For Rachel, it was important to learn anger against injustice, for she had lived many lives being pushed down by others to make her less-than-herself. That is why she needed to be the young girl. She also needed to learn that intelligence is not necessary for worth, and that is why she needed to be the retarded woman."(In Jerusalem, when Rachel was about nine, she spent a few hours a week teaching English to a neighbor's son with Down Syndrome.) Rand continued: "She also needed to learn that everyone is capable of becoming an abuser, no matter how spiritually developed, because the abuser lives within a strict world of his own ideas, and often does not see himself as an abuser but as someone being used by God to perform a certain act, or someone who is just doing a distasteful job and is looking forward to getting home and having a beer with his wife. So for her, since she is the essence that we call 'Justice,' it was necessary to accept that, although you can empathize with people's pain, and even come to empathize with your enemy, that does not mean you cannot have the right to be angry and to stand up for what is right. So, in a way, these lives were destined to show her how to stand up for what she feels is right without hating." When Rachel heard the tape of this session, she said that it really made sense.

Perhaps the concept of reincarnation feels more like a comfortable garment to Rachel's generation because they care much more about the future of the planet than do prior generations and, indeed, seem to have a special connectedness to it. José Stevens and Simon Warwick-Smith aptly summed up their perspective in *The Michael Handbook*:

> "The concept of reincarnation means that we cannot exhaust the world's supply of oxygen, nor contaminate the oceans without coming back to experience the consequences; nor can we deplete world forests and animal populations. We will live with our decisions."

And why did I feel the need to have a past–life reading on my daughter's lives during the holocaust period? It was triggered by something in Ken Carey's evocative book *Starseed: The Third Millennium* (Harper, San Francisco, 1991):

> "These next two decades will see the most rapid period of change any human civilization has ever known. To ride the currents of that great change, young and old alike will require all their native wit and sensibilities.
>
> If you care about the young people who will reach adulthood in the 1990's and in the first decade of the twenty-first century–the children who are in your schools today — share with them all the knowledge you will, but preserve their inherent confidence in themselves, for this is how they show their confidence in God."

Be merciful unto me, 0 God, be merciful unto me;
for my soul trusts in thee; yea, in the shadow of thy
wings will I make my refuge until these calamities be
overpast.

Psalm 57:1

"When you meet anyone, remember it is a holy
encounter. As you see him you will see yourself. As
you treat him you will treat yourself. Never forget
this, for in him you will find yourself or lose yourself."

A Return to Love by Marianne Williamson
Harper Perennial, 1993

XIII

Healing Time

מ My relationship with Gadi began when I moved to Tel Aviv from Jerusalem. I began to work as the spokesperson of the United Jewish Appeal (UJA) as soon as we arrived in Israel. Rachel was then six and a half years old. My decision to take Rachel and move to Israel was based on a number of considerations. I'd earlier lived there for three years and was very enamoured with the "Israeli mystique", and I thought that it would be a good place to raise my daughter. Israelis love kids in much the same way the Brits love their dogs and the Americans (and Rachel's father) love their cars. Also, I was fluent in Hebrew and had a professional background which was very impressive to the Israelis. And, finally, I'd been divorced for three years and had a bunch of girlfriends in similar circumstances, who seemed quite content to plan their lives around the latest sale at Bloomingdales and where to "do lunch", and I knew that there had to be more to life than this.

I met Manny the first day I began work at the "Kremlin", as the Jewish Agency was lovingly dubbed. He was short, slight, wiry and curly-haired, with energy that was non-stop and a heart as big as all outdoors. When we met, Manny had been divorced for a few years. But while he was married he'd had a long-term relationship with an American woman, an affair which almost destroyed his family. His daughter left home at the age of fourteen to live with a boyfriend, and it took him a few years to mend his relationship with his two sons. Manny was the one solid, loving relationship I needed after my emotionally abusive marriage. And he was wonderful with Rachel, who needed the fathering love he gave so freely. He loved me unconditionally and helped me very much to heal the scars from my marriage.

He was very supportive of anything I wanted to do, and we shared some glorious times during the four years we lived together.

Once we took a week's holiday to the island of Kos in Greece. We actually thought that we would get married there, as we could not marry in Israel because Manny was a Kohen, or a member of the priestly tribe, and I was a divorcée. In Israel there is no civil marriage — marriage and divorce matters are under the jurisdiction of the Rabbinate or religious law and, according to Jewish law, a member of the "priestly" tribe could not marry a woman who had ever been married (read: non-virgin), so may Israelis in similar circumstances marry in Cypress. So we thought that we could tie the knot, so to speak, in Greece, not realizing that just as Jewish as Israel is, so is Greece Greek Orthodox, and there is no way that two Jews from Israel could ever marry in Greece, at least not on the Isle of Kos. So, we decided to have the honeymoon without the wedding. We found wonderful, deserted beaches, went skinny-dipping, made love under the stars, drank lots of wine and, as I recall, ate lots of taramasalata. Manny was keen on taking pictures and I half-reluctantly agreed, since he promised me that he'd keep the photos in his briefcase once we returned to Israel, and he assured me that the kids wouldn't see them.

Upon our return — by this time I had opened an advertising and PR agency, and Manny was working with me — one of our clients called me with a special request. He was a young gay man who had just returned from San Francisco. "Listen," he said to me, "it's so easy to meet people in San Francisco [this was the early 1980's, practically pre-AIDS] and I'd like you to run an ad for me in the paper with your post office box number, and once a week Manny can read the letters to me." For many of us "Anglo-Israelis", speaking Hebrew was easier than reading it, especially when it came to deciphering someone's handwriting. We actually received about sixty letters — all legitimate, by the way, and some of the most poignant and heartfelt cries of loneliness I'd ever heard. Some letters were from men in prison, some were from men who had been married for years and this letter was their first tentative and brave step out of the closet, and a few were from younger guys who, as Rachel might say, "had their shit together."

One day, when Manny and I finished a client meeting and went to the car, we noticed that I had left the window open a few inches and someone had broken into the car and had taken Manny's briefcase. Manny was convinced he'd get it back, as his identity card was in it and there was no money or credit cards inside. About a week later, Manny told me that he'd heard from the military police. It turned out that someone saw that there wasn't any money inside, so he flung it into an empty field. The police then brought their little robot to ascertain that there was no bomb inside and then they opened it, saw his ID card, and gave it to the military police where his buddies from the army work, "so I'm going over to pick it up. I told you it'd turn up." And off he went. About an hour later he returned, laughing so hard he couldn't speak. "What happened?" I asked him over and over again, and finally he calmed down enough to speak: "When I got to the base, everyone there was peering out from their doors, guys I've known for thirty years, looking at me very strangely indeed...I heard someone say, 'Is he or isn't he?'...and when I went to the commanding officer, he pulled me in quickly, shut the door, and said to me, 'I've known you since we were kids; you've always had a wife or a beautiful woman in your life, and the photographs in your briefcase prove you're still a sucker for a pretty face and big tits, but then I find a bunch of letters, and I see that you're advertising to meet a man! So, buddy-to-buddy, are you straight, or gay, or bi, or what!!??'"

And so, for months following, Manny would tease me...in the supermarket, for instance, he would stop and talk to someone and then whisper to me, "He's from the base," and I would jokingly cover my breasts with my arms.

When Manny left the his travel agency and started to work with me, I began to feel smothered, simply because there was too much togetherness for my Gemini soul, which disliked routine. I now understand that part of my reluctance to commit to this relationship was that I didn't believe I deserved all the love that Manny gave, but a greater part of me just didn't love him with the intensity with which he loved me.

Manny was a wonderful lover and told me that a former girlfriend had schooled him in the art of lovemaking. Once she called and was speaking to Manny, and I asked to speak with her. All I said to her was "thank you" and all she said to me was "you're welcome." But just as an alcoholic might not be aware of his dependence — "I'll just have a few drinks after work to unwind" — so, too, I got into the habit early on of having a joint or a drink with Manny prior to our making love. When I started seeing Gadi and there was such incredible passion between us that nothing was needed short of his presence, I came to understand that the relationship with Manny had the right timing, but not the chemistry. With Gadi it was all chemistry, but the timing sucked.

Manny, who was about thirteen years my senior, was always running around organizing everyone. He seemed the picture of health, slim, fit and open. He had given up cigarettes ten years earlier and yet he had a heart attack, albeit a mild one, after we had been together for two years. Manny went into total denial, as if it never happened. I talked to him about diet, about vitamins, whatever, but he was not ready to take responsibility for his body.

About a year later I realized that our relationship was beginning to drain me. It was like a reservoir, full of water — always there when you're thirsty, until one day you go to get some water and it is empty. I think this analogy probably is true for many relationships; the love seems to be there and then one day, suddenly, it seems, the love is all gone. Actually, the very week I decided to ask Manny to leave, he had his second heart attack, and of course I was there for him and waited many months before he was well enough for me to tell him that I wanted to separate. It was not what he wanted to hear from me, but I was honest with him; I just didn't love him anymore and, with Rachel approaching puberty, his approach to parenting was very inconsistent. He would get angry with her for something minor she had done and then allow her to get away with stuff that definitely needed disciplining. I felt the need to side with Manny as a matter of respect, and poor Rachel (the essence of "Justice", according to Rand Lee) was feeling frustrated and confused. Manny suggested that we fly to Cyprus and get married, and I told him that our relationship mirrored the Sondheim song "Send in the Clowns".

Manny did not want to leave; he became needier and more clingy each day, and I remember pointing out to him, with my limited understanding of the concept of karma at that time, that perhaps this was his payback for the years that he had carried on a relationship practically under his wife's nose, causing his family great pain and distress. (He told me that he would take Dooby, his dog, for a walk and spend a few hours with his lover, who lived up the street.) But Manny was not interested in my theories; he was, as my friend Colleen would say, "in Egypt, in de Nile". He finally left, however we kept in touch. Rachel would spend the occasional weekend with him and Dooby, and both Rachel and I had cultivated a real bond with his youngest son, whom I kept in touch with. During the four years I was involved with Gadi, Manny suffered two more heart attacks and, ten months before Gadi was killed, died while waiting to receive a heart transplant. His daughter believed that her father had died of a broken heart and that I was to blame, and she specifically requested that I not attend Manny's funeral. As hurt as I was, I now understand that when her father died she was left with many unresolved issues and her pain was so great that she needed to blame someone, and that someone was me.

Manny and I had been separated for nearly five years when he died, and my roller-coaster relationship with Gadi was at a high point. Deepak Chopra has written many books dealing with the extraordinary power we all have for health, longevity and healing. He says, "When the spell of mortality is broken, you can release the fear that gives death its power. Death is ultimately just another transformation from one configuration of matter and energy into another, but unless you can stand outside the arena of change, death represents an end point, an extinction."

A few months after Manny died, another friend was killed when a small plane carrying both him and his secretary crashed in Mexico. Ehud was still in his thirties when he was killed and was, without a doubt, one of the most brilliant men I had ever met. He had served as the Prime Minister's advisor on terrorism and had played an active role in Israel's far-from-small participation in the Irangate affair. A few months before he was killed, Ehud had come over to visit. He knew that I was attempting to raise the money to buy the rights for the holocaust black comedy *To Remember, To Forget*, and he wanted to share some information regarding investors with me. Nothing sinister like arms for options, just an honest appraisal of the Israeli film industry (dismal), of the author, Dahn Ben Amotz (a dirty old man who can write), and of Israel (this country eats you alive).

He also suggested with a twinkle in his eye where I should consider living: "Moses stuttered, so his brother Aaron was designated to be his spokesman. God promised Canada to the Children of Israel and Moses tried to tell this to his brother, but because he stuttered as he tried to say Canada, he said 'Can...ca...aa' and Aaron promptly understood it to be Canaan." Less than five years later, I was living in Vancouver, British Columbia, thinking that I had, indeed, found the new Jerusalem.

During the time of Ehud's visit, Gadi was away filming in Kenya. It was not my intention to have sex with him, but somehow it happened, and it was a truly glorious encounter. Since he was the only other man I had been with in ten years, aside from Manny and Gadi, and AIDS was forefront in everybody's minds, I asked him if he had a condom which, of course , he didn't. He told me that he had not been with another woman for ages, and intuitively (and by the way he made love) I knew it was true. Like Gadi, he too was in a "dead zone" in his marriage, but when he started calling me and wanted to see me again, I told him that I couldn't handle a relationship with one married man, let alone two. A few months later, when he was killed, I felt that some foul play was involved. The Irangate affair was in the news, and both Israel and America had a lot to hide, and it was obvious that Ehud had a great deal of information that neither side wanted to be made public.

Between July, 1988, and May, 1989, the only three men I'd had sex with in twelve years were all dead. I remember feeling somewhat like Maggie from *Northern Exposure* and thinking that two men that I'd been intimate with — Manny and Ehud — both died a couple of months apart, and I wondered if perhaps I was a sexual 'jinx'. The one thing I felt certain about, however, was that with Gadi's death I had finally shut the door on any relationships with married men. Actually, I shut the door on any relationships whatsoever for more than four years. The time had come to heal, not to hump!

Set me as a seal upon your arm, for love is strong as death; desire is cruel as Sheol; its flashes are flashes of fire and flame. Many waters cannot quench love, neither can the rivers carry it away; and yet, if a man would give all the substance of his house for love, people would mock him.

Song of Solomon 8:7,8

"Sexuality connects you with a frequency of ecstasy, which connects you back to your divine source and to information."

Bringers of the Dawn Barbara Marciniak
Bear & Co, 1992

XIV

Sacred Sex

"In any case, when King Manasseh was crowned in 693 B.C., the pendulum swung back to the Goddess... in the inner sanctum... the priests deflowered privileged virgins, winners of a series of "Miss Judah" contests".

Spoon was as shocked as she could be by this talk of fornication in the Holy of Holies. Conch Shell explained to her that the First Temple had teemed with sexual activity from the night of its dedication onward, even, to some extent, when under strict Levite (Yahwist) control. A famous pair of phallic pillars guarded its entrance, and, like almost all the temples of the ancient world, it was financially supported by the earnings of holy prostitutes...

"As near as I can determine, Miss Spoon, this business had nothing in common with some sordid grinding in a cheap motel or drunken octopusing in the back seat of a car, such as you might have heard the Jesuits condemn. Why, it was even more exalted than marital congress. This was sacred sex, conducted with ceremony and in full consciousness, meant to mime the act of original Creation, to celebrate life at its most intense and crucial moment. We're not talking the old in-and-out, slip-slap here, Miss Spoon, we're talking the ignition of the divine spark...."

skinny legs and all by Tom Robbins
Bantam books, 1990

I read recently that all women fake orgasms from time to time, and I thought that there must be something wrong with me because I never have. I mean, the orgasm that Meg Ryan faked in that famous scene from *When Harry Met Sally...* was a a real occurrence for me; I always had what she was having — only louder. If we were in Jerusalem, Gadi would say they could hear me in Tel Aviv; Manny once suggested that my mother could hear me in Philadelphia! There were times, particularly with Manny, that I could almost go back to a place in time somewhere in Persia or Babylon or Egypt, and feel like people were watching our lovemaking; that it was somehow sacred, and that I was a priestess of love or something. Mind you, I was often stoned when I was with Manny, so I didn't pay much attention to these things. And yet, although nobody was talking or writing about it much, I felt instinctively that sexuality and spirituality were somehow connected.

For thousands of years, Chinese, Indians and Tibetans have apprenticed themselves to the ancient sexual art of tantra by practicing lovemaking as a sacrament. According to Hindu tradition, tantra was first embodied in the god Shiva and goddess Shakti, whose divine lovemaking was a dance they believed kept the world spinning. The word "tantra" in Sanskrit means "expansion" or "weaving', and the word "yoga" means to "join together". Tantric yoga was a partnership practice that focused on health as much as spiritual and sexual intimacy. In the ancient civilizations of Sumeria, Egypt and Greece, sacred sex was a healing act. Those who returned from war were taken first to the temples of the Holy Prostitutes where the soldiers were restored to their sense of self. Brenda Peterson, in her article "The New Eroticism" (*New Age Journal*, May/June, 1993), writes: "Each maiden in the society was asked to serve at least a day in this temple ritual. These women considered their service a sacred honoring of the goddess; it was a privilege to perform the holy arts of sexual healing. The priestess-prostitutes offered ritual bathing, cleansing, massaging, praying and purification through lovemaking. This holy lovemaking restored health and balance so the soldier could return to daily life after having seen so much bloodshed and violence and death... The ancients recognized sensuality as a life force strong enough to redeem the warrior from death's stranglehold." After I read this article I found the book *The Sacred Prostitute* by Nancy Qualls-Corbert. Her book begins: "On my first excursion to Israel several years ago, I noticed numerous little clay statues in the small gift shops of the kibbutzim and in the larger antique stores. I was attracted to these figures almost magnetically. Each had the crude form of a woman. Some were delicately molded while others were crudely formed; some depicted the entire body with intricate designs in the gown or headdress, others were simply fragments of a small head with only a suggestion of facial expression. They were not reproductions, they were originals dating back to long before the Common Era (B.C.E.). Excavated from the ruins of many towns and villages of this ancient land, they were images of ancient goddesses."

There was something about this information that had a real resonance deep within my soul, so when I went to see Rand Lee to check out Rachel's past lives during the holocaust, I also asked him if I had any connection to the Holy Prostitute. In trance he told me that I am connected to the High Priestess essence of passion and that I express that part of the divine essence connected to the "Ruach HaKodesh" or the female energy of the Holy Spirit of Passion. In Hebrew, the "Ruach HaKodesh" or the Holy Spirit is indeed feminine. There is also a Hebrew feminine word for sun ("shemesh"), moon ("levana"), and God, or more accurately Divine Presence (Shechina). He said that as the expression of the female energy of expansion, my goal is to recognize what my heart really needs and to give it to myself persistently.

Rand continued: "As you know, in Kabalistic thought the 'Ruach HaKodesh' was often seen as a female; not an entity, but a female energy of generation and expansion. And, so, in a way, you represent this. In your cluster of incarnations as the High Priestess essence you have been learning many things — belief, strategy, harmony, action, support, communication — but in this incarnation you are learning passion and you are connected to the incarnational essence of the one who enters physical reality to learn to translate her inner dreams into action, acting with proper organization and determination until you get it. You are presently entering a life cycle called 'the World of Strategy cycle' and in this cycle you have been getting in touch with your life purpose, and bringing through information and making contacts and doing networking that would be useful for your life purpose and this is why you have had so much travel, but you are entering into your next seven-year cycle, the cycle called 'the Empress of Harmony'. This is significant because the Empress is the physical aspect of the High Priestess so this is the cycle of your wealth, and of your home, and of your long-term security, and of your feeling that at last your dreams are translating into reality."

This was heady stuff. I had been feeling, for about six months, that my life was about to change, so Rand's words about getting in touch with my life purpose was totally accurate — could the wealth be far behind? Gadi's death had marked a turning point in my life, but sometimes it seemed that I was doing merely that... turning and turning, trying to catch my tail. When I returned to Philadelphia with Rachel with a promise of emotional and financial support from my parents, I discovered that that support came with conditions; i.e., renting an apartment next door to them, getting back my old position as marketing director of the Jewish Publication Society, having Rachel attend Temple University (my alma mater). So I decided, after Rachel was accepted into the theatre department of the College of Santa Fe, to move to the Southwest with her. I'd recently had a session with an astrologer who told me I'd be living somewhere surrounded by mountains-she actually thought she saw Vancouver, a place I'd never been , but for some reason was very drawn to — so Santa Fe seemed a good mountainous compromise. I just needed to heal and thought that the return to nature would be beneficial for me, and that I would be close to Rachel whenever she needed me (like when she'd call at midnight from the dorm and ask me to bring her something to eat!). After a year in Santa Fe, the mecca of US "spiritual-materialism", as I would discover, I felt the need to return to my roots in England and to begin to own my life again. It meant separating from Rachel's energy for a while. She was nineteen years old, involved in a loving relationship with Adam, yet still under the influence of my mother, whose judgement of my marching-to-the-beat-of-a-different-drummer lifestyle was in no way nurturing for any of us. And, although my mother probably doesn't even have the slightest understanding or even interest in reincarnation, the idea that your child in this life is actually your mate from a past life, having returned to give you even more aggravation, would, at the very least, cause her to chuckle. As I was about to leave, a screenwriter friend who was encouraging me to write said, "You know, sometimes you just have to jump off the edge and build your wings on the way down."

In England I was able at least to begin writing. Perhaps being back in the land of my birth helped me to be somewhat more contemplative, perhaps it was the joy of obtaining a Reader's Card from the British Library, or perhaps it was the fact that, as a British citizen, I was eligible for housing benefit and income support so that I could support my habit. The British are logical, thinking people some might call anal-retentive (particularly the men), and yet there are spiritual roots older than Stonehenge itself.

From the time of the First World War people started seeking out spiritualists or mediums to connect with their departed loved ones, and the Celtic tradition extends much further than Ireland itself. Even in Vancouver there is a monthly newspaper called *The Celtic Connection*. And the crop circles, so prevalent in England, are, according to Barbara Marciniak's *Bringers of the Dawn*, "phenomenological expressions of consciousness which have come into our reality to show us that the logical mind cannot control all of the data. The crop circles occur to intersect with the coding of consciousness of all human beings."

Whenever reality cannot be explained, a certain niche is opened within consciousness, and the crop circles are completely beyond the logical mind. "There are a number of reasons for the existence of the crop circles. Basically, they exist to force reality to move — to get you feeling rather than thinking. Most who explore these circles think their way through the circles rather than feel their way through them. Great Britain is having a rash of them because, in general, the British have a very logic-oriented consciousness. However, the land of the British Isles is imprinted with megalithic spirals and stone forms that have intensely imprinted the intuitive faculties of the inhabitants. This phenomenon has no logic to it. It is forcing a logically oriented society to recognize something that makes no sense, and it is being done in a very playful and obvious way without creating a threat to anyone's view of reality. If ships were to land everywhere, people would get upset, When corn lies down in concentric circles and it doesn't even break or die, no one really gets too upset."

My relationship with Daniel, my first relationship post-Gadi, mirrors this. Daniel is a logically oriented British CPA who, through knowing me, has been forced to recognize someone who makes no sense (he calls me "the crazy American") to his logical mind, and yet, he has begun to walk on his own spiritual path. We met when I was looking for an accountant, and in our initial phone conversation he suggested that we meet for dinner. I suggested instead that we spend a Sunday together, as there was a flat for rent in Oxfordshire that I wanted to drive up to see. When he came to pick me up one Sunday afternoon, I was struck by how very much, physically, he reminded me of Manny, and I felt instinctually that his was an old soul I'd known before. The very first question I asked him, as soon as I got into his car, was when his birthday is. It just blurted out, and it had nothing to do with astrology. Of course, he knew nothing about my relationship with Gadi. "Feb. 7," he said, and saw me go pale. Gadi's birthday was February 7! Talk about a cosmic connection, this was the ultimate cosmic joke. Gadi, the snake with the Jeff Bridges body, had sent me Dudley Moore with the compassion of Ghandi!

From the start he called me "cherub" and I called him my "special angel", and in his droll and caring way he helped me to release the demons left by Gadi. I wonder if what Ghandi had and Gadi didn't — namely the letters "h' and "n" — stand for help and nurturing — the very two things that Gadi never gave me and Daniel had an abundant supply of?

Maybe if I'd known then what Rand Lee told me some months later — that the High Priestess is an archetype connected to the Mother goddesses of my culture and that, in many cultures, the Holy Prostitute has been a High Priestess essence individual because her energy both brings life into the world and buries the dead, both at the same time — I wouldn't have needed so much help and nurturing from Daniel. After all, wasn't that the total help and nurturing package all rolled up in one archetype? Rand continued his tranced reading,

"And, because you are a high priestess of passion, you must learn that to live fully in your body is as holy a doorway into enlightenment as the spirit is [and for years I'd been duped into thinking sex was just good, clean fun, and all the while I was opening a doorway to enlightenment] and so, it is true that in Babylon you did, indeed, practice as this kind of high priestess and served the Goddess Ishtar at the Ishtar gate. Also, you have served the Goddess Aphrodite in Greece in her earlier, more primitive incarnations, and you have also worked with the Goddess Isis, although we see this as a male entity, not a female; and so, this is true that you have been a holy prostitute and so, if you ask, and call upon the high priestess or the Popess energy and ask it to come and bring back to you the memory of all your lives, exploring the goddess energy, you will have much more information, even for another book!"

Nancy Qualls-Corbett, in her book *The Sacred Prostitute*, writes that the Babylonian goddess Ishtar was the goddess of love, passion, war and death. Her sexual activity was emphasized through descriptions of her as the "sweet-voiced mistress of the gods", yet she was also known for her cruel and relentless fickleness toward her lovers. Since she was the bringer of love and sexual joy, she also held the power to take them away. "Without this tempting, full-breasted goddess, nothing that concerned the life cycle could come to pass. When Ishtar makes her descent into the Nether World, no passion is felt on earth and sterility overcomes the land. On her return to earth, life and love are awakened once again. " The sacred prostitute expressed her true feminine nature and divinity — the "Ruach HaKodesh" Rand spoke about — and her beauty and sensuous body were not used in order to gain security, power or possessions. She did not make love in order to obtain admiration or devotion from the men who came to her, for often she remained veiled and anonymous. She did not require a man to give her a sense of her own identity; this was rooted in her own womanliness. The laws of her feminine nature were harmonious with those of the goddess. By worshipping the goddess in lovemaking, by bringing the goddess love into the human sphere, the union of masculine and feminine, spiritual and physical, the personal was transcended and the divine entered in. As the embodiment of the goddess in the mystical union of the sacred marriage, the sacred prostitute aroused the male and was the receptacle for his passion. As the goddess incarnate she assured the continuity of life and love.

At the time of this reading I knew nothing of "the sacred prostitute". But, as I felt a definite link between sex and healing, I asked Rand if I had used sex for healing. "That is correct", Rand answered. "It was part of sex magic and it was also part of worshipping and celebrating the divinity through the sexual act." I thought this was terrific and had a flash of going into the "Sacred Prostitute business" and so I asked, "Will I be doing that kind of work again?" With my PR background I was already franchising the entire operation in my head, but Rand's answer was a tad less commercial: "We feel that in the work with Daniel you are accomplishing this for yourself. You must understand that through many of your incarnations you have given yourself for others, but you still have to complete healing work on yourself in this area, and the final lesson of the high priestess is to nurture yourself first, and then let the overflow of your self-nurture go to others; so that what you have done for others in the past, in this incarnation we feel that you are asked to do for yourself."

I thought about the myriad of healers, psychics, channellers, chakra-readers, mediums I'd met since leaving Israel and how some, although certainly not all, seemed to be in dire need of healing themselves, and yet were healing others. It seemed truer than true those words I saw on a "New Age" card which said: "To heal the planet you first have to heal yourself"...and perhaps, by healing ourselves, we are in fact already in the process of healing the planet. So, according to the information Rand Lee was conveying to me from the group intelligence, my relationship with Daniel was one of the healing things I was doing to nurture myself. I was learning to look within, past the external trappings of tall, fit, handsome, great buns, or whatever, and find caring, compassion and cuddles. Clarissa Pinkola Estes in her inspiring book, *Women Who Run With the Wolves*, writes: "Within the masculine psyche, there is a creature, an unwounded man, who believes in the good, who has no doubts about life, who is not only wise but who also is not afraid to die. Some would identify this as a warrior self. But it is not that. It is a spirit self, and a young spirit at that, one who regardless of being tormented, wounded, and exiled continues to love, because it is in its own way self-healing, self-mending." This is the man we women are all searching for.

Daniel's faith and belief in me enabled me to build my wings after I had jumped off the edge. Rand ended his reading with a tarot-based description of our relationship: "Your heart chakra is your primary chakra, and the root chakra your secondary chakra. You are the most physical of the high priestesses. Daniel himself is also the spiritual essence of the hanged man essence. He is in the introspection triad, you are in the nurture triad, and as the hanged man of strategy he is very balanced between the physical and the intellectual and his job is to help people find a pathway and a balance in their lives [Daniel's expertise professionally is personal and business insolvency and he has, indeed, helped many people]. The high priestess and the hanged man are often very good as co-partners because the high priestess has the heart and visionary and dreamtime connection, and the hanged man has the connection with channelling as well, but with a specific emphasis of bringing through information that will balance the spiritual with the physical. So the hanged man is good at building bridges from the dream state into the physical which the high priestess is often not good at doing. Are there any final questions?" I had none. Rand had brought my relationship with Daniel into an alignment I had not entirely understood until that moment,

What we had both been dealing with, however, was Gadi's jealousy of our sexual relationship, which he was communicating vehemently about, from the other side!

.and Saul said to her, Divine for me by the familiar spirit, and bring up for me whom I shall tell you. Then the woman said, Whom shall I bring up for you? And he said, Bring me up Samuel. And the king said to her, Fear not, what do you see? And the woman said to Saul, I saw gods ascending out of the earth... an old man is coming up covered with a mantle. And Saul perceived that it was Samuel, and he bowed with his face to the ground and made obeisance.

1 Samuel 28
8,11,13-14

"... Your father is dead," the psychic said, "Recently passed over?" My father had died eight months before. "Yes," I said. "He's all right. Your mother is grieving too much. You should tell her that your father is all right and he wants her to stop grieving so much.

Travels by Michael Crichton
Ballantine Books, NY, 1993

XV

The London Psychic

y "You have a father on the other side, a strong-minded individual; he is putting his hand on my shoulder to give Sunny moral support." Arthur Molinary is speaking to me at the College of Psychic Studies in the Kensington area of London. The date is February 9, 1993, two days after Gadi's and Daniel's birthdays. I'd been feeling for a couple of weeks that Gadi wanted to communicate with me, so I searched for the best medium in London and was given Arthur's name. No sooner did I sit down than he began to give me information from my father who had died ten months earlier. "He says he wasn't able to say goodbye to anyone; he wasn't able to say goodbye to the four of them." I was totally thrown off-track for a couple of moments. What four of them? Slowly it dawned on me. He was talking about me, my two sisters and my mother. My dad died doing what he loved, working as a supervising Rabbi in Wilmington, Delaware. During the last ten years of his life he travelled throughout the tri-state area of Pennsylvania, New Jersey, and Delaware, spending up to a week at various food plants running the gamut from chemicals and spices to yogurts and chocolates. That funny symbol on many food products, Ⓤ, actually stands for the Union of Orthodox Rabbis, and indicates that the particular product thus labelled is kosher. In his seventies, my father had discovered faxes, mobile phones, and secretaries, a world of business he had never known, and a world, furthermore, filled with Gentile people, another thing he had barely known for most of his life. During the traditional week of mourning, several people who worked at the plant had come to pay their respects to my mother and, while speaking with them, I realized how very much my father had been loved and respected by his co-workers.

They told me that they had flown the flag at half-mast, something I was to hear again, only this time about my paternal grandfather, also a Rabbi in England, who died at the age of forty from pneumonia.

My Uncle Mike, my father's only surviving brother, told me that when my grandfather died in Wallasey where he practiced as a Rabbi, the boat that carried the coffin across the Mersey to Liverpool where his body was to be buried also flew its flag at half-mast. Over the years I have heard wonderful stories relating to my grandfather, who died when my father was nineteen; that he spoke seven languages; that he was writing articles for major newspapers in Israel; that he made a violin; that he was a botanist; that the townsfolk, of whom many were illiterate, used to bring their letters for him to read and to write their replies. And, how very much he was loved.

My father, it seemed, was also very loved by those whose lives he touched, but for me, growing up as the eldest daughter of an Orthodox Jewish Rabbi, I always felt that I had to do certain things not so much because they had real meaning, but because "people will talk." When I was about thirteen, a shopping mall was built about fifteen minutes from our house. As I was about to walk over there one Saturday with my girlfriend, my father asked me where we were going. "Over to the new mall," I replied (actually, in those days I think it was probably called a shopping centre). "It's Shabbos," said my father. "You're not allowed to go there today." I argued, "We're not taking any money, and we're walking," but my father said it had to do with the "eyein ha'rah" or evil eye, that someone would see me there and say that the Rabbi's daughter was shopping on Saturday and tell everyone. Naturally I didn't buy this, but I also didn't go because I had a great deal of respect for my father.

Arthur Molinary continued: "Your father is a strong-minded person. He puts his hand on my shoulder to give Sunny moral support, something he has been doing since late November because you are working on a new project which began at that time and he has been helping you." This was unbelievable...I actually began to write this book in late November! "He has an inquiring mind; he liked honest people and he had a quick mind. You are very much like him," and, in the very same breath he suddenly said, "You know someone who was murdered." I immediately thought of Ehud and that suspicious plane crash in Mexico, so I asked, "What do you mean by murder?" "Death under suspicious circumstances," which indeed they were. "Didn't your father believe in God? He says there is a God and he now realizes that all religions are manmade; God didn't make them, we make them. He has a sharp, clear mind. Didn't he know his own father? He is now getting to know and enjoy his father. He is very interested in your new projects. If he were alive he would be listening to this reading I am giving you. He would today be a better father. He did not show too much emotion; he was more like a father-figure...he didn't give hugs...he was more like Victorian England." How could this stranger — who had met me five minutes ago, to whom I had uttered exactly six words — have known that the very last time I saw my father alive he gave me a hug, the only hug I remember ever getting from him? That hug was so full of pain and disappointment, because he was angry with me at the time, and I remember thinking that I would never see him alive again.

A few weeks before that, I had arrived in England (for my cousin Jon's wedding) a week ahead of my parents. Because I'd been travelling, I hadn't seen an invitation until I arrived in the UK, when I learned that Jon's wedding was black tie. I hadn't brought anything appropriate to wear. When I told my mother that I might rent a dress for about £50.00, she said, "Go ahead and rent it; I'll pay for it." I told my sister, "I can't believe that Mom offered to pay for the gown hire; she must think that there'll be eligible men at Jon's wedding." The following week when my parents arrived, my mother suddenly had a change of heart. "I never said I'd pay for it," she said, and something inside me just cracked.

So many promises had been made to me throughout my life which had been broken, that this was the final straw. I sat down and wrote my mother a letter citing all the times she had not come through. (I was still healing from the Gadi liaison, and feeling as if I'd jumped off the edge and might remain wingless forever.) It was not a nasty letter, it was written from my heart; but my mother was hurt and angry with me. When you've lived in denial for as long as she has and someone comes along and challenges you to be authentic, it must be a Herculean task to swallow that pill. So my mom was angry and wouldn't speak with me. My father told me that he had read the letter and that, even though Mother was hurt, there was a lot of truth to what I had written. But Mother's influence on my father was great, and when I went to say goodbye to them before they returned to the States, my dad's embrace was like a piece of plywood, and so Arthur's words rang true.

Arthur continued: "He is concerned about Sarah's blood pressure; he says it's too high." I was shocked. My mother's Hebrew name is Sarah! "Was there a bit of friction between them? It wasn't what you'd call a lovey-dovey relationship. He's very down-to-earth...black is black...white is white. He may have been a rabbi but he's very grounded." What a wonderful choice of words Arthur used. My father is "grounded" in heaven! He went on: "He's been helping you since November, which has given him quite a few months to 'sort his mind out.' There's no time on the other side...he's in full control and very eager to help you with your life, your quest and your projects. Since November he has come to terms with his 'sins' (if you can call it that), and he throws more light onto this thing we call 'truth'. He has very expressive eyes [true] and if he says something he expects you to be listening. He has that bit of a teacher that says 'I'm telling you' [the word 'rabbi' means teacher, and my dad was a teacher for many years]. He hears your every thought. He listens to your prayers. He actually comes close enough to give me goosebumps," Arthur said. "He wants you to tell Sarah that he's still alive; that his body might have gone, but his personality hasn't died, and he wants you to tell her to have her blood pressure looked after straight away."

My mother's grief over losing my father was tremendous, and I knew that she was going through a very difficult time. The thought that she might have a stroke or something really threw me. I played Arthur's tape to a few friends and my cousin Perry, all of whom were convinced, as I was, that the information coming through was accurate and credible. They all felt that my father was giving a real gift to my mother by warning her about her health. I called my sister who speaks to my mother every week, because I felt that my mother would not listen to me. "Could you please ask Mom to have her blood pressure checked." I said to my sister. "I have information that it might be dangerously high."

She immediately started screaming at me, "You've been to another psychic again! When will you ever stop with this crazy 'New Age' stuff and get a normal job and start making some money?" And with that she hung up on me. A month later my mother came to England for Passover, and I made a copy of the tape and gave it to Mom with a very carefully-worded note: "Just listen to this with an open mind...you don't even have to discuss it with me; or you can write me your thoughts...whatever you feel comfortable with. I just felt that I should share this with you," and I handed it to her before I left. Now there are many technologies in which America surpasses England, but Royal Mail in the UK is second-to-none. Next-day delivery practically throughout the entire country, and it's cheaper than the fax. And so, the very next day I found the tape in my mailbox, with the following note:

When are you ever going to accept the fact that your beliefs and mine are miles apart? Had I known what was in the envelope you handed me, I would not have accepted it. I have 51 years of wonderful memories tucked away in my heart and am dealing with my grief in my own way. I absolutely do not need the voice of a stranger on a tape to help me. I do not believe in mediums, etc., so to hear the tape would be pointless. I realize that you think you might be helping me, and I do sincerely appreciate it—but now that you know how I feel, please don't discuss it again.

(And yet, one evening, when I was staying with my folks for a few months, my mother told me to turn on the radio in my room as there was a psychic taking calls and being interviewed. When I asked her if she wanted to hear it, she said that she didn't believe in that stuff; but when I went to the kitchen ten minutes later, my mother was standing there listening to it, and quickly turned off the radio when she noticed me.) My mother was due to return to the States a few weeks after I did, but was unable to travel and had to stay in England because her blood pressure was too high. To her credit, when I told her I'd tried to warn her a few months earlier she said, "I wouldn't have listened to you." Recently, I sent her Dr. Deepak Chopra's tapes, *Ageless Body, Timeless Mind*, and she actually listened to them, so a shift does seem to be taking place (even if she fell asleep during his guided visualization.) Over the past year she's even done acupuncture treatments.

In England I met a healer who told me about the "Forgiveness Diet". It entails writing seventy times for seven days the following: "I (the name you were called as a child), now forgive (mother or father's first name) completely." Generally, women need to start with their fathers and men with their mothers. I don't understand how it works, but it definitely does work. The magical number of 70 x 7 days somehow affects the DNA and a shift takes place. It's not even important to concentrate; you can do it like you used to do in school and write "I" 70 times, your name 70 times, or any way you wish. I did it first with my father, and I felt a shift almost immediately. I felt that what I was forgiving him for was the fact that when my brother died when I was two, my father closed down and never spoke of the incident again. My mother told me that my father spent lots of time with me during my first few years. He used to feed me my "eggie", take me to the beach, and play with me. How I must have picked up his pain (and my mother's) in those early years. Is that when I started to fabricate the story of how I caused Michael's death? I don't know, but a few months after I did the "forgiveness diet" my father died, and even though I had no way of knowing that he would be communicating with me from the other side ten months later, I do know that the process helped me to deal easily with his passing. I also did the forgiveness diet with my mom, and today our relationship is better than ever.

Arthur had yet more information from my dad: "He's very excited about helping you," and then he turned to me and asked, "Have you already done two books?" I said no. "Are you sure?" he persisted. "He talks about two books." (Actually, before I began this book I spent a year researching for a book I was planning to title *From BC to AD-the Essene Experience*, but my father was never aware of this.) "He will give you as much information as he possibly can-directly through you-he says you've always had answers for every Tom, Dick, and Harry, and that you're a survivor — again he says that you've always had answers for everything and everyone." I was amazed; my father never seemed to like the fact that I often played shrink for my friends. "Is he disapproving?" I asked.

"No, not at all. Now he is preparing you to get your notes ready to give a lecture. He is preparing you now because he was never caught with his trousers down and he says 'she does tend to leave things until tomorrow' and he was always ready. He comes across as a serious man, but he also has a dry sense of humor." Arthur then said that my dad was teasing him and that he felt that he would get along with my father. "You have lots of papers and books on your bed, and opposite your bed is a window. Your father stands at your window, on the right, giving you inspiration. He has shed his judgements." The I asked if he had seen his son. "Spirit children have very little personality," Arthur explained, "which is why your father's connection is stronger with you...babies, miscarriages, abortions...all go up as pure spirit."

And then, with no preamble whatsoever, he said, "Who is Manny?" I nearly fainted! "Manny is helping you also. He is a very restless energy; he wants to be in ten places at once." Manny was such a restless energy that even when he watched a cowboy movie on TV he would be rocking in his seat as if he, too, were riding a horse. "He says you are a very bright personality, but have you been a bit flat lately? He keeps patting me on the face to cheer you up, and says you have to be on more firm ground." I was actually at that time living in "The Little House of Horrors" with a woman healer, misguided and afraid, who was involved with dark energies, and the situation was beginning to affect me. "Twice he says, 'I shouldn't have died, you know.' He says that he neglected himself. But he, too, is very keen to help you with your search. And I'm hearing a piano and he's sending you a song — it's 'Send in the Clowns'." This was incredible — Manny's name, Manny's personality, and now the song which had described our relationship — it seems I had indeed found the best medium in London.

When Arthur asked me if Manny was good at organizing, I flashed back to when Rachel and I arrived in Israel. Manny came into our lives and, through his unconditional love, helped me to find that nurturing, sensual part of me that my husband had tried to destroy. In his myth-shattering book *Fire in the Belly*, Sam Keen writes that "The average man spends a lifetime denying, defending against, trying to control, and reacting to the power of WOMAN." Arthur said, "Everyone is organizing...there's going to be a clash of personalities up there...this is going to be a very creative year for you…you must believe in astrology because Manny is giving me some information about the sun and Venus. There are five yellow floating lights…five men…what a greedy woman you are! Thank your lucky stars that you don't have to feed this lot — you'd be in the poorhouse!" So far, in this amazing reading I could count my father, my grandfather, Manny, and possibly Ehud. Would Gadi come through or had Miriam indeed been correct when she told Rinat (and Rinat told me) that Gadi's connection with me had been "purely sexual"?

After we met face-to-face, Rinat herself told me she didn't believe that; just as I came to understand that there had, indeed, been a poignant yet plaintive rapport between them. Arthur went on,

"A fourth gentleman is coming forward…shall I or not…he is very depressed…this is the gentleman who might have been murdered — is the fifth gentleman your husband? As he starts, he, like your father, left so much unsaid. His heart was good, but he didn't know how to break through his fortress which held him down and held him back. He was very quick at summing people up, like your father and you, and had great perception. He is giving you a great deal of support because he didn't when he was alive, but now he is pulling out all the stops. He is going to pull all the stars in the sky — he says 'she needs them', he calls them 'drops of magic' — one had to work jolly hard to get to know him…he's very proud of you… behind your back he puts you on a pedestal…have you ever experienced the distant kiss? That a kiss you receive from someone else is actually coming from him?

From the moment I met Daniel and discovered that he and Gadi shared the same birthday, every kiss he ever gave me felt as if Gadi, somehow, was involved. Daniel and I had discussed this, and, right before I played this tape to him he had said to me,

"You know, I really do put you on a pedestal," and when he heard this segment, he could not believe his ears.

But Arthur was far from finished: "He only loved two people in his life" and, in an apprehensive yet cynical tone, I asked, "And who might they be?"

Whose confidence shall be cut off, and whose house is a spider's web? The wicked shall put his trust in his house, but it shall not stand; he shall hold it fast, but it shall not endure. If he is uprooted from his place, then he will deny him, saying I have not seen thee. Behold, it is he who examines all his ways, and out of the earth others shall sprout.

Job 8:14-15,18-19

Now surely he would understand; but not a bit of it.

"Peter," she said faltering, "are you expecting me to fly away with you?"

"Of course; that is why I have come." He added a little sternly, "Have you forgotten that this is spring-cleaning time?"

She knew it was useless to say that he had let many spring-cleaning times pass.

Peter Pan by John Barrie

XVI

Guidance from Gadi

Arthur Molinary repeated his words, "He only loved two females in his life — one he called…I'm having a hard time getting this as it's not an English name — Lee or Li — and the other one is you!"

It actually was not until I got home that I understood of what Arthur told me. The name of Gadi's youngest daughter is Li-or (pronounced "Lee-or," meaning "my light"), so Arthur was saying that the only two females that Gadi had loved were "light" and "sun." What a revelation for me. Until that moment I wasn't at all sure if he had even loved me. But Arthur still had more to tell me: "You had to work jolly hard to open this man up. He was very closed and is very grateful that you got him opened up before he left you. He made a rude exit, didn't he? You planted the seeds. He didn't trust women, but he trusted you. He had been let down and hurt, but you gave him confidence. He went like a 'bang' — but he's still around." Then he said that there was a dog greeting me (Manny's dog, Dooby) and then asked whose birthday was this month. This took place two days after Gadi's (and Daniel's) birthday.

He continued, "He says, 'Thanks for a bundle of good memories; no one can take that away from us.' He has a bundle of sad memories too (and so do you), but you have good memories together." Then he said: "He wants to know what's different about your hair?"

I started to laugh and said, "Men! I don't know any woman — and particularly a Gemini woman — who has the same hairstyle she had four years earlier!" Then Arthur asked if I write words that Gadi was not able to express when he was alive, "for, let's face it, he wasn't one to give you words of sustenance and nourishment, and now he can because he's not so screwed up with his emotions. He was very emotionally insecure. My grandmother always said that it's better to go red in the face once from saying it than white and livid 1,000 times wishing you had said it."

What incredible feelings were going through me. Gadi, who kept everything bottled in and never spoke to me about his feelings (lucky I could "bed-read"), was now communicating with me through a medium and telling me that he was going to speak to me from the other side. True, he certainly wasn't one to give me words of "sustenance and nourishment," but I couldn't believe there was any way this could happen. It was amazing what had come through thus far, but I wasn't a medium. Heck, I'm one of those people who, when she visualizes, gets nothing. I mean, if you ask me to close my eyes and see an apple tree, I can't even do that. Nor a cherry tree. So, as impressed as I was with this reading, I thought that Arthur was going a bit over the top.

But Gadi still had more to say, and Arthur continued, "He was always expecting the worst. Life could have been so much simpler. Your relationship didn't 'relate' and now it can. He shows me a memory of him standing alone, at the seashore at sunset—he liked to be alone."

"He loved sunsets," I interjected. "Do they have sunsets on the other side?"

"There are breathtaking sunsets in the spirit world," Arthur answered. "They don't have a sunset, they have a dimming, and after the dimming it's daytime...no darkness exists. His only regret is if he could have spoken what was in his heart instead of swallowing, swallowing, swallowing. He's only loved two women in his life and his daughter is one of them."

This was something I'd be grateful to hear over and over again; perhaps, like the Little Prince seeing forty-four sunsets, I, too, needed to hear this forty-four times whenever I was sad... "The strange thing is," he continued, "he is full of enthusiasm, love, excitement, and full of support to help you with these projects."

And I thought, what a pity there's no money in heaven, that's how he could really help me now. And then he started coming through with information as if he were actually directing the film version of this book. "He says things have to be glossed over a bit more. Make the bedroom scenes pow. Have the story woven through a lot of fiction so it's more saleable and interesting to the peasant mind." And then Arthur turned to me and observed, "He does have an arrogance about him."

"He was, after all, an Israeli," I replied. "That should say it all."

That evening I went out to the garden to take a short break and there, in the sky, was a huge jet contrail going, it seemed, from one end of the sky to the other. From the time Gadi died all I had to do was merely think of him, look up to the skies, and always (weather permitting) I would see a jet contrail. Anywhere—in Israel, in Santa Fe, in England, and now in Vancouver. Sometimes with friends we would see huge V's or triple lines. Recently in Santa Fe we saw a huge cross in the sky at the very moment I was sharing this phenomenon with a friend, and so I consistently feel this is Gadi's way of communicating with me from the skies, and I am comforted.

Arthur continued, "You always knew when to give him his own space. He says you're like a tornado—he knows you like a book now—and he is going to support you in any way he can."

At that point, because I'm still in body (and intend to remain that way for a long, long time), I was impelled to ask about Daniel. Arthur said: "This relationship is five months old. He's a good psychologist. He's good at communicating, is interesting, and is very interested in you, but he likes playing games. As a relationship I have no worries, but he likes playing emotional games, like emotional blackmail. He has been emotionally castrated, so he plays games as a form of survival; it's the only way he knows." Arthur added, "He makes me laugh, so I know he's a good person, but he won't give himself fully until you have earned his trust, and he can be a bit strenuous."

I would soon discover the accuracy of his words; meanwhile, I asked Arthur about Rachel's relationship with Adam, and he said, "Up to now marriage has frightened her, but now, for the first time, she is comfortable with a man, and she is more stable. This relationship is going to bear fruit and, as she's got rid of her cobwebs, she's seeing the world a bit more clearly now...don't worry about your daughter, because she's a survivor—she knows how to handle herself. No problems there." (And indeed, three years later Rachel and Adam got married.)

He ended this session, which had been one of the most astonishing and miraculous experiences of my life, with the following: "Whatever you do this year will bear fruit — whatever you do this year will succeed. This is a good year, use it wisely. You will be doing lots of traveling. You are going to North America...you will be paying a trip to Hollywood and there is a particularly strong link with Italy. Your father asks, 'Who is Guy?' He says that Guy will 'gloss things over.' You will be leaving England, but you will be coming back... You have a good communication aura which is very active. I do see a bit of green around your tummy and that tells me you need to be on firmer ground, but aside from that you have incredible love and support from your father, from Manny, and particularly from this one I call your husband. He has lots to tell you, and you have the ability to access him yourself."

At the time of this session I had no intention of leaving England: my only link with Italy was the Italian producer Gadi was working for when he died; and Guy, a friend of a friend, was a Hollywood screenwriter I had met a couple of years earlier, a "nice Jewish boy" and someone my father would have liked.

The stuff about the "green around my tummy and the being on firmer ground" (and Manny "patting" me on the cheeks) had, I felt, a great deal to do with my living arrangements at that time. "The Little House of Horrors," as I had come to call it, was a situation my soul evidently chose to help me heal my injured psyche, to take responsibility for my life, to learn to pay attention, and to learn discernment. In *Women Who Run with the Wolves*, Clarissa Pinkola Estés writes about the "feral" woman, feral in common usage meaning one who was once wild, then domesticated, and who has reverted back to a natural or untamed state once again. She writes:

"Feral women of all ages, and especially the young, have a

tremendous drive to compensate for long famines and exile. They are endangered by excessive and mindless striving toward people and goals that are not nurturant, substantive, or enduring. No matter where they live, or in what time, there are cages waiting always: too-small lives into which women can be lured or pushed."

Since Gadi's death I seemed to be operating, unknowingly of course, as a feral woman, particularly with regard to my living arrangements...my cages.

London is known for expensive accommodation — house-shares and bedsits, landlord problems and generally no leases — all factors that contribute to a feeling of not being safe, of tenuous security. In my first bedsit in London, I was told after I'd lived there a year that my landlady's family was arriving from abroad and that the three of us living upstairs would have to move out. I found another place nearby, owned by an Israeli couple who rented out space in two adjoining houses. When I moved in, the man's wife was in Israel for the summer, and the two houses were filled with young Israelis and I met some great people. I taught them about numerology, and they taught me about alternative music, and introduced me to the mystic sounds of Dead Can Dance. Rachel had spent about six weeks with me in the first house, so the second house was for me a continuation of that young, vital and passionately soul-searching energy, this time with males–a welcome shift.

I was slowly beginning to comprehend that my own spiritual awakening was indeed of interest to others, and that slowly and very tentatively, I was becoming a teacher even while I learned from them. Israeli men in their twenties allowed me insights into their hopes, dreams and fears. They were able to communicate with an honesty that Gadi never had. And then one day the landlord's wife came home and the energy in the house shifted drastically. All of her fears, jealousies and frustrations permeated the house of this lost soul, filled with pain, and I wondered why I was there. One day I asked her husband to recommend an accountant, and he gave me Daniel's name, and soon after Daniel and I met, my landlords informed me they were going on holiday and closing up the house I was living in. They gave me three days to find another place, but at least I'd met Daniel, despite the tumultuous situation. Looking back now, I ask myself why, after two horrific living situations, did I choose yet a third. Because bad things happened in threes? Or, perhaps, as Pinkola Estés writes about the feral woman:

"If you have ever been captured, if you have ever endured *hambre del alma*, a starvation of the soul, if you have ever been trapped, and especially if you have a drive to create, it is likely that you have been or are a feral woman. The feral woman usually is extremely hungry for something soulful, and often will take any poison disguised on a pointed stick, believing it to be the very thing for which her soul hungers…

"Though some feral women veer away from traps at the last moment with only minor losses of fur, far more stumble into them unwittingly, knocked temporarily senseless, while others are broken by them, and still others manage to disentangle themselves and drag themselves off to a cave to nurse their injuries alone."

I was given Mandy's name and number for a new place but was warned, by two of the Israelis living in the house, that she was, as the English say, "a few sandwiches short of a picnic." The first thing that hit me when I got to her home was the red and black area rug in the living room (see chapter eight). The second thing was her inability to listen; the third was her anger with her ex-husband, which was downright ugly, and the fourth was her obviously low self-esteem, which often manifested as anger or indifference toward her four-year-old son, Matthew. So what did I do? I moved in, brought thirty clients to her healing practice, baby-sat for free, paid her rent and utilities, and tried to be sane in an insane environment. Actually, Mandy was more misguided than anything else, and I had a very strong connection with her son and felt that I needed to be a part of his life for however short a period I was to live there. There must have been some very important reasons for me to be there in any event; perhaps as a mirror to throw shadow on my light…or perhaps as a way for me to confront my own shadows.

When I had my session with Arthur Molinary, I'd lived there for three months, and I had stopped menstruating, which had never happened before. The very next day, I got my period, so his observation of "green around the tummy" gave even more validity to his reading. At the same time, Daniel and I were developing a sexual relationship, and Mandy started seeing a man named Colin; and somehow, as Daniel and I were tentatively trying to develop trust with one another, the Mandy-Colin connection seemed, to me, to become darker and darker.

Perhaps it was the dark energy in the house, perhaps it was Daniel's unresolved issue with trust, perhaps it was the fact that I hadn't yet released Gadi from my emotional body — I don't know, but every time that Daniel and I made love in Mandy's house I felt tremendous pressure on my shoulders, as if someone were trying to pull me away or stop me from this sexual liaison, my first in the four years since Gadi had "passed over," and with a man who shared his birthday. Daniel said jokingly, "Perhaps Gadi is jealous and is trying to separate us." A few days later we would both realize just how true this was.

To everything there is a season, and a time for every purpose under the sun: A time to be born and a time to die; a time to plant and a time to pluck up that which is planted; A time to kill and a time to heal; a time to tear down and a time to build up; A time to weep and a time to laugh; A time to lose and a time to seek; a time to tie up and a time to untie.

Ecclesiastes 3:1-4,6

"Generally, by the time you are Real, most of your hair has been loved off, and your eyes drop out and you get loose in the joints and very shabby. But these things don't matter at all, because once you are Real you can't be ugly, except to people who don't understand."

The Velveteen Rabbit By Margery Williams

XVII

Gadi Speaks

D "Gifted women, even as they reclaim their creative lives, even as beautiful things flow from their hands, from their pens, from their bodies, still question whether they are writers, painters, artists, people, real ones. And of course they are real ones even though they might like to bedevil themselves with what constitutes "real." A farmer is a real farmer when she looks over the land and plans the spring crops. A runner is real when she takes the first step; a flower is real when it is yet in its mother ste;, a tree is real when it is still a seed in the pinecone. An old tree is a real living being. Real is what has life...not surprisingly, when a woman's animus is taken up with psychic manufacturing of a negative sort, a woman's output dwindles as her confidence and creative muscle wane. Women in this predicament tell me that they "cannot see a way out" of their so-called writer's block, or for that matter the cause of it. Their animus is sucking all the oxygen out of the river, and they feel "extremely tired" and suffer "tremendous loss of energy," can't seem to "get going," feel "held back by something."

Women Who Run with the Wolves, by Clarissa Pinkola Estés

One night about a week after I had my reading with Arthur Molinary, in February 1993, I had the distinct feeling that Gadi wanted to communicate with me. It's hard to explain, but I felt that I had to sit down and write. When I have done automatic writing, it has always been me who sets the time and the place. This was different, almost as if he were "calling me" to do this, like he needed to connect with me. And so, at quarter to three in the morning, I took pen in hand

and started to receive…. "Chamudi ["sweetie" in Hebrew and Gadi's pet name for me]. This is me, Gadi, not that other stuff you get. I'm not knocking the other stuff [my automatic writing] — it's wonderful and helpful. But tell me, truly, truly fair, don't you think that people would rather read about what I have to say? Don't you think they can relate better to someone like me who's been lately in body than to all of this high-level spiritual stuff? I want to tell you everything about how it happened, how it is on what you call 'the other side' so that you can put this into your book and most important, into the film version."

A few months prior, I met Mike Hartman at a party in London. Mike was the assistant producer on "Delta Force II". He told me that Gadi had been calling him and asking for work on the production as he was already in the Philippines and that he, Mike, did not feel that he was responsible for Gadi's death. However, Gadi apparently understood differently, and this is what he told me: "I want you to tell Mike Hartman that I totally take responsibility for my involvement with the production of "Delta Force II". He told you that he does not feel any responsibility toward my death and the death of the others, but I visit him at night and I see that he is still quite depressed. Tell him to get off it and start getting back into the swing of things. He used to be such a jolly man and now he is a depressant! Tell him to get off his butt and help you with this project. I told you I'm pulling all the stars for you. You deserve it and you have a great project. This film will be even more successful than "Ghost". Wait and see! Tell Hartman to get involved and to stop being such a 'cvetch.' If he works with you on this production, he will be totally healed. Tell him this is a promise from Gadi, who knows a bit more now."

The very next day I called Mike and shared this part of the transmission with him. I heard him say, "Yes," when I read the words, "He used to be such a jolly man." Truly I felt rather stupid sharing this with Mike, whom I didn't know very well, and who might think I was totally nuts, but something quite miraculous happened after I shared this with him. He noticeably shifted. He believed that this was indeed valid information and, in fact, even started to give me some pointers on how to proceed with the film, something he had never done before.

Now that Gadi had "gotten that off his chest," he continued to give me verification regarding the session I'd just had with Arthur. "It was Ehud who came through. He was involved in some dicey stuff–Mossad, CIA, etc. Ehud and Manny and I share some very special memories of you and Rachel."

Great, I thought, the three of them are sitting up there playing backgammon and discussing my orgasms–are they comparing notes, I wondered, or were they exaggerating and boasting to one another like boys in the locker room? But, to his credit, Gadi was a bit more mature than I was. Heck, he hadn't even known I'd slept with Ehud until after he died, and he wasn't even angry!

He continued on about the special memories: "But especially me, because Manny understands now about the karmic stuff he had with you and Lois (his girlfriend while he was still maried) and how he hurt his family."

When Manny was so devastated by our break-up, I tried unsuccessfully to explain how karma works, through our relationships and such. Now, it seemed he finally understood, because Gadi continued: "We have some things in common, but he knows and understands the love that you had for me was very different." When I was seeing Gadi, Manny said that I was "wasting my time," that Gadi would never leave his wife. Gadi certainly did leave his wife, and I know that sharing this story is not a waste of time; indeed, it transcends time.

Only now, as I write his words, do I truly begin to comprehend the magic of all this. A man whom I had loved deeply for four years was dead, and after he died I found out that there had been yet another woman in his life besides me and his wife, and I was angry. But more than angry, I was frustrated — if only I could talk to him and have him explain why he had behaved in the way he did! And now it was happening… a miracle. Gadi was communicating with me from "the other side."

I continued to write his words, although it would take me many months to totally trust their validity: "I cannot begin to describe the joy that I always felt when I was with you and how very sorry I am that I could never tell you. I want you to understand that I was so fucking scared. My wife basically kicked me out — I was such an absent father and my son was already into his own life [his son was 23], my middle daughter, 15, had a special bond with her mother, and Li-or [aged 13] was my great love in that family. Now I understand how I chose such a family and how I had to learn the lesson of unconditional love for my children and for my wife. If I hadn't been so scared, I would have moved in with you and Rachel, but I felt that you knew everything and everyone and thought that I needed to be in a secret place. Rinat was loving and giving and made me feel like a teenager in the beginning, but she never had your depth, and no woman I was ever with ever had your passion. I loved it and yet sometimes it scared me. Just like in the U2 song– "And you give yourself away…and you give…" You gave me so much unconditional love and I was such a fuck to you, but don't worry, you can access me at any time now and I will help you to do this script."

As I transcribe this, I have to keep looking in the notebook it's written in… getting a few words at a time, totally different from the way I write normally. Gadi's personality was coming through loud and clear, and better yet — he was telling me what I'd always suspected was in his heart but what he was not able to tell me when he was alive. Arthur Molinary certainly got it right when he said, "His only regret is if only he could have spoken what was in his heart instead of swallowing…swallowing…swallowing." Marianne Williamson writes that miracles are created in an invisible realm, and that it is the heart space, or the absence of it, which determines whether communication is miraculous or fearful, and that silence can be a powerfully loving communication. I'd always felt when Gadi was alive that his silence was his way of keeping our relationship out of the muddy waters he'd created in his marriage. If miracles are created in an invisible realm, then this was certainly my payback time.

Gadi now said, "Do you remember you once said that I would like your father very much? Well I do. He and I have many things in common."

Terrific, now they can discuss my sex life with my dad, too, and he can amuse them with the story of how I used to take off my diaper and decorate the wall with my bowel movement! I pray that being dead means being nonjudgmental. Gadi had even met my grandfather,* who died before I was born. "Your grandfather is very evolved. I think this is your link to spirituality. End of transmission. Daniel is your distant kiss — you don't need to do anything more than kiss him, you naughty girl. He will understand."

Bloody hell, not only were they all amusing themselves with my past escapades, they were trying to stop my present ones. Gadi said, "Daniel is a very good man and we (Manny, your dad, and I) have brought him to you for help at this time. Tell him not to worry (he doesn't really), that anything he invests in this film will bring him many-fold more money. This film will be nominated for an Oscar, truly. I send you many hugs, Gadi."

I shared this information with Daniel, of course, but understandably, I don't think he believed it. He was very gracious, ever the English gentleman, but I'm sure he thought that I was deluded. I wasn't quite convinced that I *wasn't* deluding myself, to be perfectly honest.

About ten days later I again felt an impulse to write. Gadi seemed to have a thing about middle-of-the-night transmissions, but this time the information resonated more to Gadi's personality, and it began to explain many things that had been left unsaid: "Hi, chamudi. This is me, Gadi, speaking to you from upstairs. You need to know that I can give you all the information you need to finish your book and your script. You see, my desire to create a film was absolutely so great when I was alive, although I was terribly confused about how to do it. I thought that I had spiritually evolved stories like "Children of Immortality," but I was so fucking naive and I couldn't tell the story of my friends who died in the Yom Kippur War because, truly, I didn't really know the story. My ego was my motor, not my soul. Now with *Shalom My*

---

* My uncle Mike recently amazed me by telling me that my paternal grandfather, an orthodox rabbi, had been a Grand Master with the Masons.

Love (love that name!) my soul, like yours, is the motor."

What was pretty amazing was that Gadi was using terminology from the session he had had with Miriam, almost as if those four years never existed. Or perhaps like he'd been in therapy for four years (maybe he had?!).

"From this side I see many things and I want you to understand so that you will be able to create a story that is timeless. For time, as you know, does not exist here. I know that it is the middle of the night on Earth, but for me there is just the never-ending flow and ebb of time-lessness. Like when you sometimes nap in the middle of your day and wake up and look at your watch and see seven o'clock and for a few seconds feel disoriented and don't know whether it is seven o'clock in the morning or at night. Something like that. I feel that you are exhausted, so I will let you sleep."

But he didn't let me sleep. Instead, he admonished me for sleeping with Daniel. "I told you not to fuck Daniel. Daniel is a special angel meant to be helping you. Did you share my last transmission with him? I know you did, but neither one of you listened to me!"

What was weird about this was that each time Daniel and I made love, the pain in my shoulders was excruciating; truly it felt as if some-one or something was trying to pull me away from Daniel, so making love had become problematic. Was Gadi jealous? Do dead people get jealous, I wondered, or perhaps, as Arthur Molinary had suggested, Daniel was playing some sort of emotional blackmail game with me, perhaps Daniel himself wasn't even aware of it but Gadi was?

Gadi then made it very clear to me as to how he saw Daniel's role. "He is sent to you as an all-important link to help you bridge your (our) story with the big bad guys in Hollywood. He is to give you ten-derness and hugs and kisses. That is all! He and you need to step out of your egos and understand that you both have the blessings of the cosmos on your heads. Daniel is very important to these projects. More than he can imagine, because by getting involved with you it will drastically change his professional life. His soul asked for a major healing responsibility and this project will give that to him. He is about to embark on a journey greater than he could ever imagine by his help and involvement, which is pure love and compassion. Do share the earlier transmission with him. Tell him that he, like you, is full of light which is beamed down from above. His father, too, is very much around him, and has been since he met you. You see, chamudi, we all up here feel so blessed that people like you and Daniel are open to our messages, because we need the world to know that death is not the end and that the love you all show to your fellow men and fellow women — love without conditions — changes the tenor and fabric of both your lives downstairs and ours upstairs. Add to this the fact that the Earth is going through vast changes and many people will die."

Gadi's message ended with a reference to a dream Daniel had asked me about, which I hadn't understood. "The dream Daniel had is to tell him about the changes that are to come and that he, like you, is protected because he truly is a light worker and part of his mission is to understand so that he can, in turn, help others to understand that those who come to the light will not perish and those who, indeed, "cross over" during these times of transition will, if they come in love and without fear, be able to continue to communicate with their loved ones on the other side, as I can come through to you. I send you blessings of peace and many hugs."

A few days later I received information again. This time he helped me tremendously with understanding who I am and explaining why he was able to transmit through me. But what I couldn't understand was why he was objecting to my sexual relationship with Daniel. I still thought that it might be jealousy since, after all, Gadi's personality was coming through loud and clear. Ehud was dead, just like Manny, so they had no bodies. But Daniel, whom he claimed to have sent to me to help me was very much in body. He'd even made certain that Daniel and I would recognize each other by Daniel and Gadi sharing the same birthday. And Daniel was the first man I'd had a relationship with since Gadi died four years earlier. Surely he would want me to have fun. But I was still living in Mandy's house, the situation becoming more unbearable each day, and Daniel was about to do something that would nearly uproot the still-tender sprouts of our ripening relationship. Perhaps Gadi had foresight....

Fret not because of evildoers, neither be envious of the workers of iniquity, for they shall soon wither like grass, and fade away as the green herbs. Trust in God, and do good; dwell in the land, and seek after faithfulness. Trust in the Lord, and he shall give you the desires of your heart.

Psalm 37 1-4

"Teaching how to look within for the peace that must precede any true action dissolves the stress that fills our energy field and causes so much of the world's prevailing aggravation."

Feminine Fusion by Chris Griscom
Fireside Books, 1991

XVIII

Jealous and Ill-Intentioned People

In new age circles there's an entire mystique around soul mates. It derives from a searching for a deeper fulfillment in relationships, and often the dream of meeting one's true "other half" can get tangled and confused with old identifications or imagined archetypes which one person might awaken in another. Daniel shared Gadi's birthday, but our romantic connection came about too quickly. We should have developed the platonic relationship before embarking on the sexual relationship. Perhaps many of us are learning that it is a process, to have relationships only with people who are able to reveal themselves totally so that we can know them both inside and outside; then we can break past our own fantasy projections and begin to reconnect to the universe. Marianne Williamson, in *A Return to Love*, writes:

> "If your heart's desire is for an intimate partner, the Holy Spirit might send someone who isn't the ultimate intimate partner for you, but rather something better: someone with whom you are given the opportunity to work through the places in yourself that need to be healed before you are ready for the deepest intimacy."

When Mandy began intercepting my mail, cashing my checks, and finally disconnecting my phone line, I knew that it was time to leave. Since I was soon to depart to the States, Daniel arranged for me to move into a bed-and-breakfast near his office. I'd applied for a new passport, since mine had expired, and was told by the passport office that they had sent it to Mandy's address. Daniel said he would pick it up for me, along with a few items I had left there. He was aware of the situation, and I asked him to please not discuss anything about me with Mandy. I was so happy to be out of the dark astral energy of that house. He, an avid Tottenham Spurs fan, said he was on his way to a soccer match, would be at the house for five minutes, and not to "get my knickers in a twist" over Mandy. I asked him to please not talk about me with her. I was very clear about that — I felt that she had behaved despicably and wanted nothing to do with her whatsoever. I'd received a clear message from my automatic writing before Gadi passed over to" be mindful of jealous and ill-intentioned people."

And so, three hours later when he called and informed me that he had been with her all that time, that after making him dinner she wanted to go into trance to have her guides "clear up the situation," and that he had agreed, I was livid. Whatever had come through was total bullshit and Daniel knew it, but I felt that he had not honored my wishes. I was angrier than I had ever been in my life and allowed myself to express it for the first time in my life — immediately, not weeks or months later. Clarissa Pinkola Estés, in *Women Who Run with the Wolves*, says that it's a mistake for others to think that just because a woman is silent, it always means she approves of life as it is, and that there are times when it becomes imperative to release a rage that shakes the skies, but it has to be in response to a serious offense against the soul or the spirit. When women pay attention to the instinctual self, they know when the time is right, and they act and it is right. Right as rain. To make matters worse, Mandy told Daniel she hadn't received the passport, when the passport office informed me that indeed it had been sent to her address. They issued another, but that took weeks to obtain.

So I was angry with Daniel for what he had done, with Mandy for her dishonesty and manipulation, but mostly I was angry with me for the drama I had created. As Marianne Williamson says: "If we're frantic, life will be frantic. If we're peaceful, life will be peaceful. And so our goal in any situation becomes inner peace. Our internal state determines our experience of our lives; our experiences do not determine our internal state."

At that time, I hadn't yet the wisdom of Williamson's book *A Return to Love*, but I did have an open line to Gadi. I turned to my notebook and tuned into my dead lover, the man who had broken my heart; only now, it appeared he was helping me to heal.

"Chamudi, I know you are thinking that Daniel doesn't 'deserve' me to come through you to speak with him. [That was exactly what I was thinking!] Perhaps you are right, but only if you are planning to work this through without compassion. You, sweet Sun, have evolved tremendously over these past months because you are learning the lesson of forgiveness. Daniel is a dilettante and is thus trying to find his way. Do not begrudge him his search...he will find his way home. Do not be angry with him for going to Mandy. There is a curious naïveté about him and yes, Manny says that he has a strong Libra influence which causes him to want to be everybody's friend and to be loved by all."

Six months later Daniel sent me his astrological chart, and he does have both Saturn and Neptune in Libra, both in the 7th House. The 7th House is associated with the concept of "others," people other than ourselves with whom we are involved in such a way that they influence the progress of "how one projects oneself into the world." Neptune in the 7th House indicates karmic ties in marriage or partnerships. According to Daniel's chart: "Often there is a strong psychic link with the marriage or romantic partner, and in general a strong intuitive awareness of other people. People with this position can be easily affected by the moods and feelings of others. If Neptune is well-aspected, spiritual values are applied in relations with others, manifest as unselfish love and understanding. The ability to understand others may be intuitive. A well-aspected Neptune can indicate an ideal spiritual marriage, but if Neptune is afflicted, these natives can be confused and misled by other people."

Gadi continued: "Do not think that he is trying in any way to hurt you, for he is not. It is true that, as Arthur Molinary told you, he does use emotional blackmail and perhaps this situation arose for you to become aware of this tendency, for we know that you cannot abide any kind of manipulation. Daniel's tendency is to sometimes play both ends against the middle (he is, after all, an avid fan of sports) and you can only move to the sidelines and request 'time out.' His 'peace of mind' which he so longs for will only come when he learns to go into his own heart for the answers to the meaning of life. For he knows everything...he just needs to remember. It would be helpful for him to start to practice meditation on a regular basis."

This was good advice not just for Daniel but also for me, and the process of meditation has brought me peace, love, and joy — inspiring me to utilize my talents for the good of humanity.

"This will enable him to go within in order to get the answers to the questions which confuse him. Also there is some important information from his father, and it would help him a great deal if he would indeed go to Arthur Molinary for a session."

The message from Gadi continued, "And you can tell him that if he truly wants to know where you are coming from, all he has to do is sit quietly for five minutes and ask Spirit to give him the answers he seeks. Also the time has come for him to deal with Daniel. In many ways his life is just beginning, and we see so much potential. He does listen to you, but that caution causes him unnecessary stumbling blocks."

Daniel's Moon is in Pisces, which indicates a "supersensitive emotional nature which acts like a psychic sponge, soaking up the thoughts and emotions of others. This extreme impressionability on the unconscious level makes the person feel psychologically vulnerable, with the result that he withdraws into seclusion to protect himself emotionally."

When I first met Daniel, he had just gone through a major business trauma, and as he slowly began to heal he called me his "good luck charm." We, like most people in a new relationship, found ourselves in a situation of tremendous force and intensity. A new love relationship is exhilarating, and we want to open up without reservation. Yet, at the same time, we come up against inner cautions about letting go. We ask ourselves questions like: "Can I really be open with this person? Can I trust this person? Will she meet my needs? Can I live with what I don't like about him? Can he/she accept me as I really am and really be there for me? If not, could I be too badly hurt?" And since most of us have been hurt before, it is natural to ask these questions. If we just let our passion override our caution we could be asking for trouble, but if we allow the fear to close down our hearts, we will never find out what a new relationship has to offer. This pull between love and fear undermines the love, for it destroys the tension between the self and the other, known and unknown, that love actually thrives on.

Gadi suggested I move to the sidelines and request "time out." I've chosen my sidelines 8,000 miles away from Daniel and have experienced an ongoing healing process. I have learned that some of the most powerful and penetrating moments in a relationship are those that bring us to an edge — where heaven and earth begin to connect with each other inside us. That was exactly what I was experiencing with my new "relationship" with Gadi — his love had taken me into an unknown territory and I needed to process this extraordinary gift I had been given. The time had come for me to leave England, at least for a while. I was still hurt over Mandy and what I saw as Daniel's betrayal.

Gadi had something to contribute to that scenario as well. He said: "We understand how very violated you feel regarding Mandy. The most important thing for you to understand is that she still has many fears and therefore you, who have shed yours and can walk fearlessly toward your bright tomorrow, make her feel jealous and insecure. We know that you have helped her a great deal, but you should not feel badly that she has taken your money and your passport. You know that you are on your way to a much bigger and brighter tomorrow and that the Universe always pays back. Be grateful that you are out of that strenuous energetic situation. Now that you have left, you have freed yourself, and by the end of this week your plans will be forming for you to take off. Daniel will help you through this situation. Do not be sad. Truth and justice always triumph over deception and dishonesty." Gadi who had deceived me and been so dishonest when he was alive was certainly seeing things from a new perspective.

A few weeks before I moved out, Mandy told me she was pregnant and how thrilled she was. A few weeks after I left, she'd had a miscarriage. Everything that Gadi was transmitting to me turned out to be correct, and some of it certainly helped me understand how different the perspective is from the other side.

"It is very easy for me to now see who is attached to greed and money and how these attachments are based in fear. I was the King of Fear and my crown was money, so now I can look down and see how many people are misguided just as I was. It's funny, now I live in a place where money does not exist and where all needs are met. It is glorious to be in a place where there is no fear, although I wish I could be with you now that I understand that LOVE IS ALL. For knowing this over here and knowing that you have learned this on your side give me a yearning to be able to touch you and to be able to give you all that I did not give you when I was alive."

As I write this I can't help but wonder what might have happened to me and Gadi had he not been killed, and I am struck by the fact that it is only the truth that set Gadi free — the truth that we are immortal beings, that death is only a transition. And of course, because when he was alive he was so very fear-based, it was his death that also freed me. It would be pointless for me to say, "If only he could have expressed these things when he was alive," because his soul's mission was to experience physical death and to communicate to me from "the other side," to "get it" and then explain immortality to those of us opening up to the possibility of life after death.

Actually, had Gadi lived I believe that he would have moved in with me and Rachel, that I would have remained in Israel, and that the same pattern he created of cheating on his wife, on me and on Rinat would have continued. I once gave him a birthday card that said: "You are a prince, a hero, a gentle one who brings me Camelot." But before the prince can save the damsel in distress, he has to slay the dragons that surround her castle. So do we all. These dragons are our demons, our wounds, our egos, and our brilliant ways of denying love to ourselves and others. I believe that Gadi's dragon was slayed on May 16, 1989, when the *Delta Force II* helicopter crashed in the Philippines. For those of us still in our bodies, the letting go of fear is a process. We have to root out the patterns of our egos and detox them from our systems before the pure love within us can come forth. Gadi's death has liberated me, opened me to the wondrous magic of immortality, and so I have come to believe in the magic of enchantment and in miracles. I have come to understand that love does not die.

A Course in Miracles says that our holiness reverses all the laws of the world. It is beyond every restriction of time, space, distance, and limits of any kind. When Gadi was alive he believed that he had so many problems–money problems, relationship problems, work, sex, death, –when in fact he had only one–denying love. Denying love is always the only problem and embracing it is the only answer. It had taken Gadi's "passing over" to show both of us that it is only through the miraculous power of pure love that we were both learning to let go of our past history and begin again.

Gadi concluded his transmission that night with:

"How glorious were our times together and still I held back; the fear that my wife would find out, the fear that I wouldn't be able to support two families, but you, you sexy thing, you never held back and I was always amazed and pleased (and flattered) by your openness and lovingness. I cannot be with you yet, but you know that your orgasms are a small death and bring you that much closer to me. Oh yes, I, too, experience your utter joy and abandonment–it is but a small gift, but one that we can both enjoy."

Heady stuff, to be sure, but in the months that followed I was to do lots of both soul-searching and researching…perhaps both are the same…going inside to remember what I have always known and have merely forgotten. All I knew then was that it was time for me to move on. Gadi's message ended with these words: "You must get to North America as quickly as possible; you will find exactly what you need in Santa Fe." Gadi, the sorcerer.

My last night in London, which I spent with Daniel, was magical. We no longer had a ménage à trois, and I asked Daniel how it felt not having a dead guy in bed with us, but I suspected that part of the reason was that Daniel allowed himself to respond with his whole heart for the first time. After all, I'd be leaving the next day…I was really looking forward to seeing Rachel and hoped that our two-year separation would have had a positive effect on our relationship.

A few days after I arrived in Santa Fe, Gadi had something to say about Daniel and Rachel: "Hi, chamudi. So here you are in Santa Fe. I told you that Daniel would help you. And his help has only just begun. I cannot say that I am totally thrilled with the way your relationship has changed, although you guys have really been making glorious music together of late. Watch the stars. You will see many miracles manifesting from now on. Your path is laid out for you; all you have to do is follow the yellow brick road of your soul map. You know how very much I loved Rachel when I was alive. Now I can see that she has developed into a magnificent being. Tell her to stop worrying about so many insignificant things. She is destined to be one of the leading light workers of the coming decades, and there is a purity and a clarity of vision about her that she needs to keep finely tuned at all times. Her grandfather is constantly guiding her, and he wants her to know that he is very proud of the magnificent person she is becoming."

It was true; when she wrote on her birthday note to me that I'd helped her actualize herself, and when I met with her professor, and just in spending time with her, I realized that she had grown to be a compassionate and, as Gadi said, magnificent person. She was living with Adam, her friend Shawn, and various and sundry cats and dogs. Rachel and Adam were both actively working on their relationship and growing up.

I felt very strange in Santa Fe, as if something was slightly off. In the two years I'd been away, it seemed as if everything had doubled in price. I sensed a lot of fear and some very strange energy. Although according to Condé Nast, Santa Fe, New Mexico, is the second most popular tourist spot in the world (San Francisco is their #1), there's lots brewing below the surface of the awe-inspiring natural beauty of Santa Fe. Four distinct groups live in Santa Fe: the Native Americans, the Hispanics, the artists/new age community, and what I call "the burn-outs." The last group has been growing over the past few years. These are the people, often from California, generally wealthy, who came to live where the real estate is attractive and the air is rarefied. And there's very little intermingling. Probably the only time the entire population got together was when the Dalai Lama came to town.

Also, there's no industry whatsoever in Santa Fe, save for government and tourism, which doesn't help matters. Then there's Los Alamos, a short ride from Santa Fe, where the atomic bomb was developed. And yet, there is a goddess energy here so strong that one cannot help but feel it in some way.

When I came to Santa Fe in 1994, everyone was raving about the sessions they'd had with a woman named Beth Hin. I was "psyched out" and said, "She must be Santa Fe's flavor-of-the-month," until I heard my friend Michael's tape. I was impressed; it was as if she were speaking to his soul — the vocabulary, the points of reference were tailor-made for him. "Maybe I'll go see her," I said to Michael, whom I was staying with. "Forget it," he told me, "she's super-booked; people are waiting months to see her; since Christmas [this was the end of May] she's seen 700 people Santa Feans need lots of healing." (I was reminded of the joke I'd heard when I first lived there. Question: "Why did the Santa Fean cross the street?" Answer: "Because she was channeling a chicken.") I was halfway finished with this book, I was thinking about a movie based on it, but I had no idea where to go. Vancouver still beckoned; I had Daniel's backing and belief, along with a commitment from UK director Peter MacDonald, but I was at loose ends. As it happened, Beth came over to Michael's one day for a haircut, and Michael introduced me to her. "I'm writing a book and intending to produce a film," I said. "I know," she answered. "I need to see you. Can you come to me tomorrow?" Even more incredible than my ability to access Gadi was the session I had with Beth the very next day. I was finally about to understand the significance of the spiritual path I'd chosen.

Blessed is the person who finds wisdom, and the one who finds understanding. For the merchandise of it is better than the merchandise of silver, and its gains than fine gold. Wisdom is more valuable than precious stones; and there is nothing to be compared to her. Length of days is in her right hand; and in her left hand riches and honor. Her ways are ways of pleasantness, and all her paths are peace. Wisdom is a tree of life to those who lay hold of her; and blessed are those who wait for her.

Proverbs 4, 13-18

XIX

Shining My Light

When I went to see Beth the next day, I was unprepared for what I received. Daniel's financial backing was tremendously appreciated–although he believed in what I was doing, he didn't understand it, or me, for that matter. There were friends in England who were giving me moral support, to be sure, but the UK, and London in particular, was living through a tough recession and the fear was present from Soho to Southgate, an ever-growing cloud of doom and gloom. And since it is our thoughts which create our reality, I was ready to change both. Daniel was doing well as a certified public accountant...there was something akin to "chapter eleven" in the UK, and he was really helping people with their personal or business insolvencies. And he was doing it with integrity and compassion, both of which he had in great supply. I said to him that it was truly ironic that the people I'd approached to invest in this book said no because they were holding onto their comfortable lifestyle and were frightened to take a risk and had now gone bankrupt and therefore compensating Daniel who was then able to help me. Of course, they weren't the same people I'd approached, but I couldn't help being struck by the divine retribution of the situation.

In his brilliant book *The White Hole in Time* (Harper San Francisco 1992), Peter Russell tells us that:

"The last thing our present economic system wishes to see happen is that we wake up and realize that we do not really need most of what we buy. It does not want us to realize that there are better routes to inner satisfaction than continual consumption. This would remove the motor from the economy. Could this be the reason why our materialist culture seems unwilling to take spiritual development seriously? ...Society is caught in a vicious circle. Our assumption that material well-being is the path to inner well-being underlies our love of money. Our love of money leads to an economic system that must maintain this illusion... It is not 'money' that is the root of all evil — as is commonly misquoted–but 'the love of money.' And our love of money is itself but a symptom of a deeper error–our addiction to the world of things."

Peter Russell could easily have been writing about Gadi when he was alive, and his belief that having one million dollars would change his life. Surely not the same Gadi who transmitted, on April 7, 1993:

"It is now very easy for me to see who is attached to greed and money and how those attachments are based in fear...." And the next day, the *Observer* quoted Gary Sinyor, co-director of a currently hot film, as saying, "If you tried to make a "Ghost" here in Britain you wouldn't succeed because nobody would give you the money to do it."

So here I was, writing a nonfiction ""Ghost", not knowing at all if I was on track, sitting with Beth Hin. "The first thing is that you are very much trusted by the heavens," she began, "so therefore the film, therefore the writing has matured and just your sensibilities about things. I would encourage you not to 'tone yourself down'; don't feel that you have to make yourself so that other people can understand you. Your greatest gift is this tremendous female power that you have...You're becoming one of the real matriarchs, so you have to let that shine."

I was in shock upon hearing these words. Practically everyone I knew, including my mother and sisters and a number of my friends from before I moved to Israel, were unable to figure out what I was about and judged me according to their own criteria. My spiritual quest was leading me to a place where the "shoulds" ("should" be earning lots of money, "should" be setting my cap on a rich man, "should" not allow my daughter to have a relationship with a "goy") no longer served me, and whatever I was being told I "should" be doing was merely the projection of their own minds, hopes, and fears. Beth said that I am needed by the heavens to come into a real fullness, and that my brother's infant death resulted in the invalidation of my sensitivities.

Beth said that my image has been, "Even if I use my sensitivity, there can be death of my 'old friend,' because I don't express what I have to say adequately or appropriately, or in a way that can be heard." And then she said, "But you just have to say it, and who can hear it can hear it."

That validation, together with Rachel's beautiful birthday note to me, was pure music to my ears. She said that there was an imprint between my first and second chakras caused by an anxiety of being put down for these acute observations; that they would be inappropriate or not comprehended or not out of a space which people would perceive as loving or understanding. So when someone is saying, "This is who I am," I say, "Ah, but let's go to that next step" because, (according to Beth) I challenge people to be authentic, as I challenge myself. In our Western culture women have been taught to fight, not to join, to find competition rather than likeness, and to say "that woman has beautiful blond hair, mine is like this," and this starts a duality which causes friction and pain.

But the main reason Beth said she wanted to see me was to explain to me about the opening of my heart chakra into enlightenment and awareness. In my case, all the channels were open except the one on the left side of my body between the first two chakras, which had not been adequately sustained by women, a fact that she found most interesting. The left side of our bodies represents receptivity, our feminine energy, our mothers, and women. She said: "I think that men have not quite known what to do with it, but they've said, 'Isn't she wonderful...such power, such courage, such love,' so they've been amused." And that made sense. Gadi, Manny, Daniel, my dad, and the other men I've known well would probably agree with Beth's reading.

She explained more about the friction and pain caused by the duality of women. "Native American women have said that this is our culture's greatest problem, that although there are many men working on a spiritual level, it is the very powerful way some of the women teachers are working that bring about unity over and over and over again. Every once in a while one of us will have something that we're dealing with that's a very intense karma and we'll feel the friction in our own nervous system, and what happens is that the other women have absolute good faith and are with us as we go through it. And so, we're to be harbingers for women in general and you are to be the one out there in the business world, and on that level there's a way in which there's to be what's called a 'feminine transmission of light' from me to you — it's not on what we call the personality level...it's on a level out of the divine."

I was overwhelmed. Beth was telling me information I'd expect to read in one of Shirley MacLaine's books! When she told me that by November I'd be "God-realized," there's my voice on the tape asking: "God what?" She gave me the prayer I'd need to ask for:

"I want that perfect alignment between my masculine and feminine sides. I want to become a realized being, an awake being, completely — as a woman, fully present."

Then she said that I will find a peaceful acceptance of myself and, more than anyone, my father will be really happy. She said that he has a "great sweetness," which of course he does. It's just that when he was alive, at times I felt that our relationship, like so many relationships, was highly conditional. Much of what we call love is highly conditional if we really stop to think about it. It's conditional upon the way a person behaves, or how they look, or what they do professionally, how much money they make, what values they profess or, perhaps, how much they agree with our beliefs or perhaps how much they appreciate us, and the more they match our expectations of the "perfect person" the more we love them and the more they become special to us.

Yet, according to Peter Russsell, "All this specialness is just a form of judgment. We have judged them as fascinating, sensitive, wise, kind, honest, good-looking, fashionable, sexy, humorous, selfless, artistic, intelligent, understanding, or whatever else appeals to our ego-mind. We have judged them as someone who will satisfy our needs. Unconditional love, on the other hand, does not depend upon how a person thinks, feels or behaves... "

Beth said that so much of what I am dealing with in my work is perfect unity, perfect love. Joan Borysenko, in her passionate and exciting book *Fire in the Soul: A New Psychology of Spiritual Optimism*, writes that going beyond duality is freeing the stuck soul, and that our soul gets stuck when we get stuck in our stories and can't move on. This is where past-life regression comes in...it can help us get unstuck from a repeating rut by making us conscious of how we got in that rut in the first place. My soul, when I went to see Beth that day, was not stuck so much as it needed some acknowledgment from this modern-day soul rescuer.

Of herself, Beth said: "People want to see totems within me—if they come through, they will be all the animals of the world, and they will be all white...My form is not particularly important. I like sweet friends...I'm just a common woman...I like chocolate and flowers and the piano...very simple things. Yet there is a universal energy that I am completely unified with, and you are coming into that space in yourself."

Beth is what is called a multidimensional being. (Actually we're all multidimensional beings, while some "way-showers" like Beth have conscious memories of their other lives.) Beth is the incarnation of Sri Sarada Devi, known as Holy Mother, the wife of Sri Ramakrishna and his helpmate. Holy Mother's last message, three days before her death in 1920, speaks to me quite profoundly and actually shows me what I have been working toward since Gadi's accident:

"If you want peace, then do not look into anybody's faults. Look into your own faults. Learn to make the world your own. No one is a stranger; the whole world is your own."

Beth said that I'm so powerful that most women teachers would meet me and say I'm wonderful where I am ("and you are," said Beth) and I replied "Yes, I know, but I want this breakthrough...why can't I find it?" She said that if I turn to women who are capable in the outside world, they aren't living from that awakeness. They, according to Beth, are living from their second and third body powerfully (that is powerfully in their mind and spirit) but not adequately in soul.

"I can't think of a woman out there in the business world who's also out there on that level," Beth said to me. "I'm sure there are several out there, but they're probably dealing with the same struggle."

It was one thing for me to get information from Arthur Molinary about Gadi and Manny and my dad, or for Rand Lee to go into trance or read the tarot cards and tell me that I'd been a sacred prostitute or that Rachel had three simultaneous lives in the Holocaust. Or even for me to access information from a "dead" Gadi. But Beth Hin was presenting me with a mirror of my own power, and it was something that I had never owned before.

I'd been put down by so many people I knew, judged because I was challenging them to be authentic, or I was patted on the head, told that I was adorable but terribly misguided, told by my sister that I was a bad influence on her kids (because they asked me what I thought about death after my dad died, and my truth was far from hers). And when I told my mother when my dad died that I really understood what she must be feeling, having lost a man I loved also, she snapped at me, "Don't be ridiculous…Gadi was married…," thus dismissing my relationship with Gadi in six words. Last year, complaining of a particularly cold East Coast winter, she said, "I'm really concerned about your father lying six feet under the snow."

Beth then said that there is a particular transmission of awareness or understanding that I need so that as I step out into the world, I can carry a certain strength and a certain cohesive understanding, and that I need a transmission from a level of insight and perfection to hold me as I work at these universal levels.

"You have it from your father," she said, "from this lover who died, from different friends who love you deeply and who have been of many traditions, but there is another level of a 'paternal training' that has to come from a consciousness that was embodied in a male…and this is the second person who will be working with you for about two and a half years. His name is Sri Yukteswar and he was Yogananda's teacher."

I'd never heard of him and I asked, "Is he alive?" She told me that he is no longer in body, that he lived in Puri, below Calcutta, and was noted for his noble spirit and was known as a Yogi of Wisdom, and that I could read about him in Paramahansa Yogananda's *Autobiography of a Yogi*.

According to Columbia University Press, "There has been nothing before, written in English or any other European language, like this presentation of yoga," and indeed the chapter dealing with the mysteries of life beyond physical death is dazzling. When I got the book, I saw that Sri Yukteswar, Yogananda's teacher, lived from 1855 to 1936 (and that Beth, in her previous incarnation as Holy Mother, would have actually known him!) and had eyes (photo p. 98), that could penetrate the very core of my being with a loving kindness that leaps out from the pages of the book as well as a wisdom that is indescribable. When I showed my friend Michael Yukteswar's picture, he said, "He looks like family," and this man called "Incarnation of Wisdom" was to be my guide for the next two and a half years!

The transmission from Beth was astounding. She explained that when a high being loses someone, they go through a grief that is not so much from the attachment as it is the resolution of the cells and the body and life into a different stabilization, and that my dealing with the loss of Gadi and my father is wonderful.

She said that I was ready for a home base, that I've had some lifetimes in the fjords of Scandinavia and through the British Isles, along the northern coastal areas of Denmark, and that Vancouver and British Columbia offer the West's answer to something I have known for centuries; so your power goes, "Ah...I can rest here. I can listen to myself long enough so that I can act out of complete surrender to who I am." She said I needed to be in a place like that because I've been in so many places and I'm soothing everyone else and healing everyone else and wondering, "When can I take a rest?" According to Beth (to whom I had not even mentioned Vancouver, by the way), Vancouver is the place where I can take my rest and begin to nurture me.

But first, I would have to face the fears still rooted in my childhood she said, and I was about to recreate that drama within weeks of arriving there, something I needed to reconcile before I'd be able to say, "Ah, I can rest here."

And he has put a new song in my mouth, even praise unto our God, that many shall see it and rejoice and trust in the Lord.

Psalm 40:3

"Perhaps the dragons in our lives are princesses who are only waiting to see us act, just once, with beauty and courage. Perhaps everything terrible is, in its deepest essence, something that feels helpless and needs our love."

— Rilke

XX

Never Ending Cough

T "There was once a prince who wanted to marry a princess. According to his mother, the queen, she had to be a real princess, very much like herself. So they traveled all over the world to find one. They traveled to the east.

They traveled to the north. "A real princess can take small, dainty bites and never asks for seconds,' said the queen. 'This princess is too greedy." So at last the prince and his mother returned home. The prince was sad that they were unable to find a real princess.

One evening during a terrible thunderstorm there was a knock at the palace door. Standing there was a princess. She was soaked, and water spilled out of her shoes and sleeves. 'I am a real princess,' she said, and the queen started to laugh.

'How can you be real when you look like that? Stay for the night and we'll discuss it in the morning.' The queen had a plan. She hurried to a guest room and stripped the mattress from the bed. She laid a single pea on the bedstead. Then she took twenty mattresses and piled them on top of the pea. She piled twenty feather beds on top of the mattresses. Now the bed was ready for the princess. 'This is where you are to sleep tonight,' said the queen. The princess was very tired. 'I'm sure I'll sleep well on so many mattresses.'

In the morning the queen asked, 'Did you sleep well?' 'No!' said the 'I tossed and turned all night. My body is covered with bruises this morning!' The queen gasped. 'You didn't sleep? You must have felt the pea. Then you are a real princess.' And so the prince married the princess. The entire kingdom was invited to the wedding."

The Princess and the Pea, by Hans Christian Andersen

"It's this thing with the princess and the pea," Beth said to me. "The princess would have been expected to come out and hold court, and all the while she is being tested by the prince's mother, and she is so tired. You are going to be needed simply to be present and be full, so that your quiet joy is your greatest gift to humanity. In terms of living, Vancouver is the place for you, and that's where you are to somehow go. I would say Vancouver's the place where your home can be and possibly a lover who would be a strong companion. You're ready for a home base and there's an energy there that will hold your soul…it's the place, the energy, and how everything comes together. A lot of it is because it's time for you, and a lot of how you will be drinking things in from that world will take care of you so that in a very unconscious way your own inner voice will start speaking. The reason that you've been doing so much traveling and feeling unsettled is that you were looking for those last two knots in your psyche to be resolved, and they'll be completed almost totally by November."

And so, with Beth's words resounding in my ears, I made my way to the Pacific Northwest. Vancouver was more beautiful than I'd ever imagined. A spectacular, modern skyline laced with newly constructed high-rise buildings. A broad harbor at its doorstep. Towering mountains as a backdrop, a rare blend of urban sophistication in an unspoiled outdoor setting…I lucked out with a summer sublet in West Vancouver, on Bellview, just half a block from the beach and overlooking the Lion's Gate Bridge. It was amazing; the flat was furnished very similarly to apartments we'd lived in in Israel. Color schemes, furniture placement, even the tapes and CDs — everything there helped me to feel that I'd come home in more ways than one. A few weeks after I arrived in Vancouver, Rachel came to visit me — she was on her way up to Alaska to spend the summer with Adam in Fairbanks.

Although it had been only a few weeks since I'd last seen her, when I drove over the border to Bellingham, Washington, to pick her up at the bus station, I was struck by how very thin she appeared, almost anorexic by a Jewish mother's standards. Did the fact that she was living in New Mexico, in a desert like climate, no ocean or significant water body, perhaps contribute to what may be a lack of negative ionization? I'd recently read that we always feel better near the sea or a waterfall or any form of "moving water," and that well-being is due to the action of certain forms of energy by which we lose electrons in a positively charged ionization, and gain electrons in a negatively charged one, like at the beach. She loved Vancouver, and almost immediately she started eating and feeling and looking 100 percent better. When she'd become an "overnight vegetarian" at the age of seventeen, I wasn't really thrilled. Like so many of us, I'd grown up in a home where meat or chicken was served every night, and fish once a week, and I told her that she wasn't getting enough protein. However, I've come a long way since then and have picked up some marvelous vegetarian recipes along the way. Our two-year separation had added a perk — Rachel really appreciated my cooking, and her gratitude knew no bounds.

Unfortunately, old patterning is often hard to break, and Rachel and I got into a fight. The next day, which was the day I was driving her back to Bellingham, this time to the ferry that would take her to Adam and Alaska, I woke up with a cough and thought that the flu was about to follow. I picked up Louise L. Hay's *Heal Your Body*, looked up bronchitis, and read the probable cause: "Inflamed family environment. Arguments and yelling." Aha! I said to Rachel, "It's because of you that I'm getting sick." "Bullshit," she answered. And she was right. Rachel left, but my cough didn't.

All through July and August I coughed. And at the most inappropriate times. My cough became the "Nader Raider" of the New Age, appearing like a veritable Geiger counter whenever I experienced some sort of healing work. The first time it happened, I was invited to hear someone "channel the ascended masters," but I arrived in the middle of a meditation. Within a few minutes I was coughing so badly that I went outside until the meditation ended. The woman, who was teaching people to read auras and not "channelling the ascended masters," told me that I shouldn't have left, that it is important for people to learn to meditate and not be distracted by outside interference. I'd just figured that twenty-five people had each shelled out ten bucks, and not to be disturbed by a never-ending cough. Since then I've also learned that it is spiritually inappropriate to charge money for meditation sessions.

On my way to Vancouver I'd spent a few days with a girlfriend from Phoenix, and we spent some time in Sedona, Arizona. Sedona is quite the powerful vortex location, and I was very affected by the place. Rachel and Adam also spent time in Sedona and had a similar reaction. So when I heard that a healer from Sedona had moved to Vancouver, I called him immediately. He lived just a couple of blocks from me and invited me over "to meet a few of his friends" that evening.

When I arrived, I saw that he was holding a meditation evening and charging ten dollars admission, a fact he'd forgotten to mention to me. Anyway, the meditation started, and so did my cough — big time. I had to leave. But not before he told me he'd like to do a healing on me, where upon I only coughed more. I later found out from a friend who did go to him for a healing session that he tried to have sex with her during the session. My coughing continued. I coughed all night, I coughed at the most inappropriate times, and I wasn't getting better. Louise Hay says that the probable cause of coughing is "a desire to bark at the world – 'See me! Listen to me!'" But why did I feel I wasn't being listened to? Why couldn't I stop coughing?

One day after I'd been coughing for nearly two months, I was speaking to a girlfriend on the phone. "You know," I said, "I remember my mother telling me that when I was a little girl I was coughing every night for a year, and no one knew what was wrong." They thought it was asthma, but it turned out that I was allergic to feathers, something no one figured out for a whole year. I'd been sleeping on a feather mattress and, although there was no pea underneath it as for the princess who was real, something was keeping me up all night–both then and now.

"What are you sleeping on?" Isabella asked, and I walked with the cordless phone into the bedroom. My summer sublet came complete with a feather duvet and four feather pillows! And then it hit me...I'd recreated my early childhood in England in Vancouver, BC. Both places were on the water, and I'd felt safe in Vancouver just as I'd felt safe as a little girl in Wallassey up until the time my mother went to give birth to my brother Michael. Having no conscious memory of that period, it did seem logical that my coughing every night would have come about after Michael died. Logically, the events leading up to the so-called asthma seizure should have occurred after Michael died. I called my mother and asked her when, exactly, these events had taken place.

"Oh, you were just a baby," she said.

"Was I still in a crib?" She said yes. "What exactly was I allergic to?"

"Your mattress; you'd been sleeping on a feather mattress."

"Wasn't that a mattress you'd have on a bed and not on a crib?" I suggested, and she said yes. "Then," I said, "it follows that I was sleeping in a bed, so it must have been after Michael died and I was about three."

"Get rid of the feather duvet and the feather pillows and you'll be fine...had you told me that you were sleeping with all those feathers, I'd have known immediately what was causing your coughing attacks," my mother said. I promtly went to The Bay, bought foam pillows, and exchanged the duvet for blankets.

And I still coughed. I began to think about that little girl as if she were both part of me and separate from me. Through the years I had been unconsciously working toward healing my heart, along with the intellectual healing I'd been doing. An important piece of the puzzle was given to me when my mother revealed that I was the one who told her that Michael was crying and that, since she was getting ready to go out that evening, she didn't come down to the garden where he was in his pram. And my father was sitting in the garden, reading the paper. I wonder why he didn't hear me. My God, I was a two-year-old child, and the hurt and the pain that I had not been acknowledged, that I hadn't been listened to, created a story that made me responsible for the death of my brother.

Now I was ready to glimpse that three year old who was coughing her heart out, who was saying, "I'm so frightened...I don't want to be here", now I could take her out of that bed, remove all her feather bedding, give her a new mattress, new cover, and tell her that I love her and that I would be back to see her in a week. I wasn't able to do more than that the first time I met her, but it seemed important that I commit to another visit.

But there was something else I was intuiting about this little girl, something I'd not realized until now. She saw that her brother was crying, but she saw more — she knew that something was wrong and she ran to get her mother who was on the phone, and was shooed away. Perhaps she ran down to the garden again, this time to witness her bother Michael's soul leaving his baby body and floating up... up... up. And now her mother comes down and her father comes over and their son is no longer breathing and her mother is screaming; perhaps in her anguish she shouts at her daughter, "Why didn't you call me?" and her father is putting his mouth on the baby's mouth, trying to get him to breathe; and now he takes the still, small body of her brother under his arm and runs to the doctor's office. And then her mother goes into a deep depression and her father never speaks of the incident again, and over forty years pass before she can put the final piece of the puzzle in place.

Rachel's drama teacher, Ruthi Dychas, brought *A Course in Miracles* to Israel. We spent an evening together at Ruthi's, and everyone chose a miracle card. Mine said,

"What could you not accept if you but knew that everything that happens—all events, past, present, and to come — are gently planned by One whose only purpose is your good?"

I just came across these words again yesterday, and suddenly I understood that God's in his heaven and all's right with the world.

A week after my first visit to my inner child, she was waiting for me again. I asked her what she wanted, and what she definitely wanted was to have fun. And so, I took her to the fair and when we got there we looked at all the rides, then we rode the merry-go-round together; all the while I held her hand, then I bought her cotton candy, a teddy bear we named Oliver (Ollie, for short), and finally a purple balloon. I took her back to her home, told her she was a divine child and very, very much loved.

It was a beautiful September day and I felt wonderful. I drove to Lonsdale Quay, one of Vancouver's fabulous farmer's markets offering a kaleidoscope of fantastic fruits and vegetables, sumptuous seafood, and unexpected treasures. When I went to get a cappuccino, a man and woman who were having a cup of coffee placed their baby daughter in her carrier right atop the counter. She was a beautiful baby and—wonder of wonders, miracle of miracles — tied around her little wrist was a string, and at the end of that string was a purple balloon! My divine child had emerged! The next day I did some body work and asked Karen to concentrate on the area between the first and second chakras. And from that moment I never coughed again.

And I, Daniel alone saw this vision; then he said to me,
Fear not, Daniel; for from the first day that you did set
your heart to comprehend so that you might stand
before your God, your words have been heard, and I
have come in response to your words.

And many of those who sleep in the dust of the earth
shall awake, some to everlasting life and some to shame
and everlasting contempt. And those who have done
good and those of understanding shall shine as the
brightness of the firmament; and those who have
turned many to righteousness shall shine and stand like
stars forever and ever.

Daniel 10
7,12
12:2,3

XXI

Never Ending Spirit

ש Beth told me that there's a tremendous amount of the Christ force energy (energy of love and information) coming into the planet, and some very amazing things will be unfolding, such as eighteen teachers being born now and over the next few years, and they're coming through at this time so that we all can move forward. Beth said it's like eighteen Dalai Lamas coming into the world at once! Each one will be working in his or her own forte, and when Beth shared this information with me in June of '93 she said that three had already been born, one in India and two in the States, and that one of her jobs is to watch over these children and how they unfold. "Their parents," she said, "will know who they are from the time they are born so that thread of consciousness is not lost, so that if that a child says, 'Mommy, the baby's crying in the pram,' the parent will say, 'that's my holy child saying that.' So that even if the parents are caught up in their own stuff, they have a frame of reference for how to deal with that enlightenment. They don't have to be enlightened themselves, but they have to know that there's a jewel of the divine that they are caring for and have responsibility for."

Beth then said that my being an effective healer, counselor, and teacher in this era is due partly to the fact that I went through the effect of loss of consciousness in my family, and stayed awake. The session with Beth was extremely healing for me; she was bringing to my awareness things I had not yet recognized in myself.

I'd gone through a sort of trauma during my prior stay in Santa Fe, which actually caused me to write this book, when I did something to my back… nothing major, but painful. After a week I took an alternating hot and cold shower to ease the pain, and then, suddenly it started, the most excruciating pain I've ever known. It was eleven a.m. on a Saturday, and I was in agony. I called a chiropractor who'd been recommended and got her answering machine. My pain was so intense that I couldn't remember my phone number! I was all alone and couldn't move from my futon, although I must have gone to the bathroom by crawling ever so slowly on my hands and knees once or twice. By midnight I wanted to die; the pain hadn't abated one iota.

According to author, Joan Borysenko, "Dark nights of the soul are extended periods of dwelling at the threshold when it seems we can no longer trust the very ground we stand on, when there is nothing familiar left to hold on to that can give us comfort. If we have a strong belief that our suffering is in the service of growth, dark night experiences can lead us to depths of psychological and spiritual healing and revelation that we literally could not have dreamed of and that are difficult to describe in words without sounding trite." I didn't know that I was going through a dark night of the soul, but at about one a.m., after fourteen hours of pain worse than labor ever was, I said something like this aloud: "OK, God, I'll write this story. I'm willing to commit to telling my story and Gadi's to the world if I can get some sleep and wake up without pain." And soon after that I fell asleep. When I awoke the next morning, I was pain-free. Not even a twinge remained…I could have jumped hurdles…well, almost.

A short time afterward I had an awe-inspiring dream where I was meditating (actual meditation was not yet easy for me as I'd have a hard time quelling my thoughts) and I was totally relaxed… I was lying on some sort of cot…and suddenly I felt beams of light — pure and Godlike — were seeping into my very being. It's hard to explain as it's so rare for me to remember a dream, but when I woke up and looked in the mirror, I was practically glowing and I looked about twelve years old! The book *Bringers of the Dawn* says that:

> "everything that you are doing, including eating a pizza, is bringing you in a divinely perfect way to that place. At some point you will understand the importance of every event in which you are participating and the integrity of the whole. In the movie "The

Karate Kid," the kid is very impatient while learning karate. He finds a master and doesn't think he has found a master. He is given things to do that he thinks are a waste of time. He does not understand that each piece he learns makes up the greater whole. You are like this kid...Those of you who are tremendously knowledgeable decided to incarnate in the species to empower it by being an example for the rest who cannot do it for themselves. You make new pathways of being as you broadcast who you are."

As I type these last two lines I now understand that I am one of those, but when Beth told me that I'm "one of the people who has created this Era coming and that the Divine is absolutely aware of this and thanks" me , I didn't yet understand what was being said to me. Beth gave me the opportunity to claim who I am, and her encouragement and acknowledgment would give me the courage to start to recognize and own my power as I asked for "that perfect alignment between my masculine and feminine sides in becoming a realized being, an awake being — as a woman — completely and fully present."

She told me that by November '93 my prayer would be answered, and indeed, Beth was correct. In May she'd said to me: "I see this once in a while, people who have been the pillars of this New Era, so thank you. People think 'that person, they do this or that, they're neat but...' and I go no, this person has been one of the pillars of God who said, 'No, consciousness is all right, I don't know how to find it, but I'm going to go for it...I've got this destiny and I can't stop it, because so much of what I'm dealing with in my work is perfect unity, love, and consciousness."

In October I had a dream that brought home with a bang Beth's information about the channel on the left side of the body. I dreamed that I was at a doctor' office — a female gynecologist, she is very sweet, she is nice. She tells me that she needs to do a "small procedure"–no big deal. All is well as she preps me. When she clamps me down and starts to get me to relax, I suddenly understand that she is about to do something obtrusive...something that will hurt. I ask her if this will hurt and she says, "Yes" and I say, "You didn't tell me...I won't have it done," and she says I must, and I say no and I scream and resist. I don't have it done. I don't allow women to cause me any more pain. What this dream did was free me. It showed me that when we're caught up in the past (or worried about the future) we're not free. When we're worried about what other people think of us, or when our need for security makes us anxious, we're not free. And whenever we judge someone on the basis of anything other than their true essence, our thinking is not free.

During my session with Beth, I asked her about Daniel. I'd been a bit concerned that in his professional capacity of dealing with people and their businesses that had gone belly up, he was picking up their fears and that, since he is so sensitive, it was affecting him. "He's a wonderful guy," Beth said, "and he treats his work very matter-of-factly...this is the world and he sees his work as something he comprehends. The Divine utilizes him to take care of these things, and he has a character that can handle that; he can create that separation so that it doesn't affect him."

Beth remarked that she'd seen so many bodyworkers carrying so much stuff in their emotional bodies, and then she sees one who's crystal clear, someone like Daniel, who can work with all sorts of people, and it just goes by them. She said that as he is integrating I will come to know in the next two years whether or not I want to have a really deep relationship. Daniel, she said, is contemplating this, and it means a great deal to him. She said he'd known before he met me that the sense of home and partnership was important, but that the combination of mental, physical, and emotional understanding that we share is new for both of us; there is a very great sympathy between the two of us so that he feels comfortable by the totality of what I am. It's a matter, Beth said, of Daniel deciding how much he wants this totality and how much he wants that quiet life he's known for so long "because with that CPA mind, it's very orderly — everything is just this way. One always has a cup of tea at ten a.m., and you live in a more spontaneous manner which he finds charming, but he also goes, 'Wait a minute — am I locked into my own molds?' so we'll see what happens since you are coming so much into your own. He is great in working with finances because he has the internal understanding and the external savvy...just put any financial issues connected with your projects in his hands, and because he loves you, he will make sure that everything is handled with ethics, appropriatenes, and communication."

While living in London, I heard Barry Norman (the UK's Siskel and Ebert rolled into one) speak on TV about director Peter MacDonald, who'd worked closely with Barbara Streisand as director of photography on several of her films. (Incidentally, "On a Clear Day You Can See Forever", starring Streisand and Yves Montand, deals with reincarnation with great depth, humor and compassion.) I called Peter, and as soon as I'd told him about this project he gave me Gadi's name. Peter had directed "Rambo III" in Israel and Gadi had worked with him. I sent him the first ten chapters of this book, and his response was, "This story begins where "Ghost" ends," and that he'd like to direct the film version of this story.

Actually the film "Ghost" ends with the words of Patrick Swayze who says, as he goes into the light: "It's amazing, the love goes with you." Gadi's reentrance into my life from beyond the veil has proved this to me beyond the shadow of a doubt. "We can convince you of many things, but it is difficult for us to convince you that you do not have to die," writes Barbara Marciniak in *Bringers of the Dawn*. Does Gadi know this now? Perhaps more than anything else, this is what he has been trying to explain in his transmissions to me. It does seem fitting that Gadi be given the last word:

"...The planet Earth is such a glorious planet. You all have your bodies, those wonderful temples of the soul. It is a blessing to be in body and to also have a mind and a spirit. I have only a mind and a spirit, but I have constant joy, something I did not have when I had a body. But you guys have the potential of having it all, once you truly understand that love is all about letting go of fear."

Between Our Worlds

Who are you, Emmanuel, and why?
You know who I am.
I am the voice of your remembering.

I am You, beyond the physical costuming,
beyond the walls of forgetting,
beyond the illusion of darkness.

I take no other form.
I claim no other identity. I use my name
because names are essential in your world.

Would you have come to hear me
if I had said, "I am you?"

There is nothing I know that you do not.
My task is to help you remember
what you have forgotten. And why do I exist?

I like the "why".
I exist by the very miracle of love.
We ARE. There is no other why.

Emmanuel's Book II Bantam Books, 1989

Epilogue

"There are many who are gazing in now and learning from you; through your eyes and through your being. Those who have passed from this Earth since 1975 are being given the opportunity from the astral world to finish what they term to be their lessons, to tie up the loose ends and to wind out the wheel of karma from the other side of the veil. This is a dispensation for assisting souls in their evolutionary process. It has never been offered before. Many times you will feel a presence. You will feel those whom you knew, for they are with you. Your feelings are valid. Bless them. Invite them to learn with you. Teach them what they did not learn before. They too are here to be your teachers. For you are each students and teachers."

Pamela Strumbough
Connecting Link Magazine, Issue 21

What was in that channeled message I gave to Gadi from Miriam as a birthday present in February 1989? What words made him ask me to take him to Miriam for a session, an act totally out of character from the Gadi I knew? For now that I finally have a translation, I realize that that message was the pivotal point of all that was, all that will be, and all that is for the creation of this tale. When Miriam channeled this she had not yet met Gadi and, as a matter of fact, knew nothing about him. And this is what she transmitted:

"An image shrouded with diverse thrills, with contrasting forces—sometimes it is hard for him to distinguish and separate them. Colorfully unpredictable emotional storms sometimes overshadow a more rational response.

"He has the ability to do, to realize ideas and dreams, with which he identifies strongly. Full of imagination, he sees a picture as it is being created, and goes for its realization. He's not afraid of effort, even at the expense of his inner strength; at times he feels a great exhaustion which is hard to escape. Therefore, it is extremely important for him to have an ideal before his eyes as a reinforcement. The knowledge that this ideal exists, however remotely, gives him great energy. Sometimes he feels that life is too big for him. The forces in him are quite contradictory; it's hard for him to create on his own initiative, to take responsibility…connected very strongly to roots.

"All the same, freedom, space, flying, and imagining attract him like magnets. He regards connections with people as highly important, and he wants to be recognized and appreciated, to be a bit above the special, to be loved and accepted. He is quite closed, although he manages to appear otherwise. He wants to have a woman of secrets, a discreet woman he can count on and share his decisions and initiative with.

"He finds it hard to make unequivocal decisions. Schedules can put him under a great deal of pressure, sometimes overwhelming him, but usually activity will pull him out again.

"He is a very dynamic man on the move. He loves children, relates to them, he will do anything for them, and finds it hard to detach himself from them. Three years ago he had an experience that has changed his entire life [perhaps that lightning storm in the Congo when he said 'OK, so we'll die'?]; lately, as well, he's been going through an uneasy period despite his activity and despite the affection and sympathy he receives. *He is facing the most important time of his life*. He'll want to make a very significant change that will include all the important aspects of life—he knows it and becomes more and more aware of it. He hasn't yet made the decision and he's still vacillating; even when he feels resolved, after some time he backtracks and overturns his own decision.

"The connection with you means a lot to him as an anchor for his soul and the sense of security he needs so greatly; despite the constant presence of people around him, the point of aloneness always exists, and he wishes to fill it. From the first moment he met you, he immediately recognized the essence and importance of the connection, and therefore this has been a dilemma for him.

"Time is no obstacle in your relationship, despite appearances — there are often delays, and there's both a purpose and a message in challenges that repeat themselves. At its core this is a courageous connection — vital, constructive, and unifying. You don't need to rush the rhythm of its essence or its changes by altering its external framework. Rushing will do no good and might even bring the opposite reaction. True, you think you're not rushing, but subconsciously you are."

The information was right, of course. I was subconsciously wanting Gadi to be with me, and of course I didn't understand then the cosmic meaning of our relationship or, how I was, indeed, to become an "anchor for his soul."

Another thing... when Arthur Molinary told me that I could channel Gadi, that he had "lots to tell me," in truth I had already heard from Gadi two years earlier. The date was January 15, 1991, eight months after he passed over and a few days before the Desert Storm action. I was understandably concerned about the situation, and I sat down to do some automatic writing. Three days before I received the information about Gadi working to keep the balance in the Gulf War, this is what came through:

"Know this: Your access to us is always available. Why do you not understand this? Why are you so frightened? We have been here for you, guiding you, since 1977, and still you do not totally trust in our message. You must understand that we have bestowed upon you a gift which is possible because you are such an open vessel. This is guidance such as you can receive from no other source. Please understand that we want only your best and nothing more. Such guidance can totally change your understanding and give you the ability to accomplish things beyond your wildest dreams! All roads are open to you at this time. Do not intellectualize, but be ruled by your openness and your feelings. It is not always necessary to question these things, for have we not told you, over and over again, GO WITH THE FLOW."

And then, the strangest thing happened. I distinctly felt Gadi's presence (as I had with Pumpkin the cat in Tel Aviv, nine days after Gadi died). In fact, I'd been feeling for a few days that Gadi wanted to communicate with me, and I'd mentioned to a girlfriend that perhaps I should look around for a medium in Santa Fe. She responded with: "Sunny, with all due respect to Gadi, he's only been 'dead' for eight months and I've read the high-level stuff you access and Gadi can't be that high yet, so I'm sure you can access him yourself." Suddenly the handwriting changed from script to block letters, and the style was exactly as Gadi spoke in English. At that time I was working on the film treatment of this story, and writing a book was not yet on my agenda. This is what came through on January 15, 1991:

PLEASE UNDERSTAND THAT I AM EVER WATCHING AND DOING MY BEST TO HELP. YOU MUST CONTINUE TO PUSH THIS BOOK. IT IS VERY IMPORTANT AT THIS TIME. WHEN I SPOKE TO MIRIAM ABOUT A TERRIBLE PREMONITION I HAD ABOUT WHAT IS GOING TO HAPPEN IN ISRAEL, IT WAS THIS VERY SITUATION WHICH I WAS REFERRING TO. YOU ARE RIGHT — I READ YOUR THOUGHTS — ISRAEL HAS A REAL LACK OF TRUE SPIRITUALITY. I KNOW BECAUSE I WAS CAUGHT UP IN THE MATERIAL WORLD AND I DID NOT UNDERSTAND, UNTIL I PASSED OVER, THAT NOTHING IS MORE IMPORTANT THAN LOVE. AND FROM LOVE COMES SERENITY, PEACE, AND UNDERSTANDING. THERE WILL BE A WAR, BUT NOT ONE SO TERRIBLE AS YOU ARE FEARING. BUT ULTIMATELY IT IS GOOD, BECAUSE FROM THIS WAR WILL COME A REAL UNDERSTANDING OF PEACE AND HAR-

MONY, BOTH IN ISRAEL AND OTHER COUNTRIES AS WELL.

ISRAEL IS A YOUNG SOUL COUNTRY AND SO SHE IS STILL LEARNING THE LESSONS AS A CHILD DOES IN GRAMMAR SCHOOL. BUT SHE WILL GROW UP VERY QUICKLY WHEN SHE BEGINS TO UNDERSTAND THAT IN ORDER TO GRADUATE TO HIGH SCHOOL SHE MUST LEARN THE LESSONS OF LOVE, PEACE, AND HARMONY. THIS IS WHY YOU ARE CONSTANTLY BEING HELPED, BECAUSE THIS STORY YOU ARE TELLING HAS REAL MEANING FOR THE WORLD AT THIS TIME. YOU ARE BEING GUIDED TO THE RIGHT PEOPLE, AND IT WILL HAPPEN.

I AM BUSY HERE, BUT I WILL ALWAYS BE AVAILABLE TO HELP YOU WITH THIS PROJECT. MIRIAM IS IN CONTACT WITH ME FROM TIME TO TIME AND I WILL LET HER KNOW ABOUT OUR PROJECT. YOU KNOW, CHAMUDI, THAT THIS WAS THE PROJECT THAT HER GUIDES SPOKE TO ME ABOUT IN TEL AVIV.

ONLY NOW DO I UNDERSTAND HOW VERY PURE AND LOVING YOU FELT TOWARD ME, WITHOUT COMPROMISES, AND I AM ETERNALLY GRATEFUL FOR YOUR HELPING ME. WITHOUT THE HELP OF MIRIAM'S GUIDES, MY TRANSITION WOULD HAVE BEEN MUCH MORE DIFFICULT. YOUR SOUL KNEW WHAT WAS GOING TO HAPPEN TO ME IN THE PHILIPPINES, AND SO DID MINE. I WAS FIGHTING IT ALL THE WAY. WHEN YOU CALLED ME IN MANILA, I WAS MEAN TO YOU BECAUSE YOUR LETTER STRUCK A CHORD, AND ON A CERTAIN LEVEL I KNEW THAT I HAD BEEN 'SHITTY' TO YOU. AGAIN, IT WAS ALL CONNECTED TO MONEY: IT SEEMS SO STRANGE TO SAY THIS NOW, FOR I HAVE SEEN A BEAUTIFUL LIFE IN WHICH MONEY DOES NOT EXIST. IF YOU HAD RECEIVED THE MONEY FOR YOUR FILM PROJECT, I WOULD NOT HAVE GONE TO RINAT. I WOULD HAVE COME TO YOU.

I DID IN MY WAY LOVE RINAT, BUT IT WAS BECAUSE SHE MADE ME FORGET MY MORTALITY, WHILE YOU WERE A MIRROR TO MY IMMORTALITY AND I DID NOT WANT TO LOOK.

YOU GAVE ME SO MUCH UNCONDITIONAL LOVE, AND I WAS SUCH A FUCK TO YOU. YOU ARE APPROACHING A BRAND NEW LIFE THAT WILL BE FILLED WITH LOVE AND SUCCESS. THE LOVE THAT YOU GAVE ME AND THE LOVE THAT YOU GIVE ME DO NOT GO UNNOTICED. BE HAPPY. BE JOYOUS AND BE AT PEACE, FOR ALL IS UNFOLDING EXACTLY AS IT IS MEANT TO. I WILL BE HAPPY TO GUIDE YOU IN ANY WAY I CAN. WE HERE ARE NOW QUITE BUSY TRYING TO AVOID A MAJOR CATASTROPHE IN THE MIDDLE EAST. YOU MUST SEND LOVE AND LIGHT TO ISRAEL. I MUST GO, BUT I SEND YOU LOVE AND LIGH,T AND TOGETHER LET US WORK FOR PEACE IN ISRAEL AND EVERYWHERE ELSE.

Figuring that I had a direct toll-free line to him, I tried to access him on his birthday, three weeks later; however, not Gadi, but my guides came through with the following short and sweet message: "Re: Gadi–today is his birthday (February 7). He has lost all connection to time as you know it and is working, along with many others, to restore the balance of light in the Middle East. He says: 'This is better than any army reserve duty I ever did. And I love you.'

So, when Arthur Molinary told me that I had the ability to access Gadi directly, why was I so surprised? Because I wasn't ready, because I didn't trust the source, and because I did not yet understand that all souls were created to be thoughts within the mind of God. As I was stretching to a higher level of connectedness with my soul energy, it accelerated. It's all part of the process of opening up and releasing old thought patterns; and it's comforting to know that people who judge our judgment either don't comprehend the process or feel it triggering the release of their own issues. Gadi, in that first transmission, was a mirror to my immortality, and I did not want to look.

Kevin Ryerson, in his book *Spirit Communication*, states that to understand the soul we first need to understand the workings of God, "for in the beginning there was but that one spirit, and that spirit folded upon itself, creating the beings who became known as souls, created in polarities — male and female — yet were androgynous in nature." The entity John the Essene speaking through Ryerson continues:

"Soul mates are individual souls with whom you were created many aeons past, for the one spirit that is God did not wish his children to be alone, but rather created you in pairs to give witness to each other's existence. Thus, soul mates were created and given charge and command to be co-creators with God. This is the purpose and function of souls, to be co-creators within the physical universe you know and see, as well as throughout all the dimensions and orders of time and space, and even beyond those levels into the projections of consciousness itself."

It seems that Gadi and I were destined to become co-creators in those other dimensions of time and space, although the memories of Gadi and our times together when he was still in physicality whisper to me of a bonding that was out of time and space. All that has happened in my life since that fateful helicopter crash has brought me to a place of joy and wonder. I now understand that I am a child of God, that Gadi is a child of God…that we are all God's children.

Before leaving Santa Fe in 1994, I had a session with Rand Lee and gave him a picture of Gadi. In trance, Rand said that Gadi is being reincarnated in a period when industrial space colonization is taking place. He said that the area is in the north, in a cold climate, with lots of fir trees. "It looks like Finland," he said, then added:

"This person held a lot of the seeds of the future in him. There is a habitat which is warm inside and a great feeling of excitement that something is about to happen with spacecraft, because there is an airstrip. It is the turn of the century, sometime between the years 2000 and 2030. He is female and wanted to be born in a period when humans are pushing off the planet. His parents are scientists."

At the time, I thought it fitting for Gadi to come back as a female. What a karmic coup — now he'd understand the grief and pain he'd caused us all: his wife, Rinat, and me. But lately I've come to understand just what's meant by being aligned with our male and female sides. It means that the female side, which is the intuitive and nurturing side, needs to work in tandem with the male side, taking action on our intuition. It's the ability to listen to that all-knowing inner voice — the voice of God, which is our voice — and acting on it in a way that reflects total integrity and unconditional love. What a magnificent future awaits all of us as we begin to live our truths.

Still in trance, Rand had a message for me from Gadi:

"Remember, the seeds of the future are being planted in your presence. You are one of the people planting these seeds. There is hope for humankind — we are not going to annihilate ourselves—because I am in the future and I am witnessing the proof that there is hope."

Then Rand said that Gadi feeds me dreams and will be feeding me inspirational flashes of the future. Rand said, when he came out of his trance, that he had never before received such a clear and positive picture of the future.

I'd actually forgotten about this session with Rand Lee until a few days ago when I sensed — for the first time in months — that I needed to communicate with Gadi and he reminded me. He said:

YOU ARE ABSOLUTELY SOWING ALL THE RIGHT SEEDS — YOU ARE SOWING SEEDS THAT HAVE BEEN GIFTED TO YOU. PLEASE SHARE RAND LEE'S FUTURISTIC SESSION WITH ME IN FINLAND — IT IS SO. I HAVE SEEN IT… I HAVE LIVED IT… I AM LIVING IT. THIS IS WHAT IT MEANS TO BE MULTI DIMENSIONAL. YOU WILL SOON UNDERSTAND. PLEASE PASS THIS MESSAGE ON. THE WORLD IS SLOWLY BECOM-

ING A PLACE OF LOVE AND LIGHT AND LAUGHTER, AND THERE IS GRATITUDE FOR THE BEAUTIFUL WORK THAT ALL THE LIGHT WORK-ERS ARE DOING. BE HAPPY, BE JOYOUS… BE AT PEACE. SHALOM.

In Memorium

SHALOM

"...It means a million lovely things,

like 'peace be yours', 'welcome home'.

And, even when you say 'goodbye',

if your voice has 'I don't want to go' in it,

say goodbye with a little hello in it.

and say goodbye with 'shalom'.

— Music & lyrics, Jerry Herman
from the Broadway Show *Milk & Honey*

Gadi Danzig
born: February 7, 1944
passed over: May 16, 1989

About the Author

Sunny Ariel was born in Liverpool, England. She holds a BA in English Literature from Philadelphia's Temple University. She started her career on Madison Avenue and has created promotional and publicity campaigns for a variety of clients, including Finnair Airlines, Vidal Sassoon, and Leonard Bernstein. She then held the position of Marketing Director at the Jewish Publication Society. Later, she formed an advertising and public relations agency in Jerusalem and published a weekly newspaper in Israel.

Her life changed drastically in 1989, when her lover — cinematographer Gadi Danzig — was killed in the helicopter crash during the filming of "Delta Force II" in the Philippines. She began to examine the very core of her existence and question what death really is. Today she is a literary agent and publicist for a number of metaphysical writers worldwide. She currently resides in Lafayette, Colorado – "The oatmeal capital of America" – with her 20 pounder black cat Money and Toulouse, a partial Himalayan.

כל העולם כולו
גשר צר מאוד
והעיקר לא לפחד כלל

The entire Universe
is one narrow bridge —
and we must learn
to cross it without fear

— Rabbi Nachman of Breslov (1772-1810)